The Betrayal Knows My Name

5

Hotaru Odagiri

Yuki Giou
A first-year high school student. In his previous life, he was a woman and Luka's lover, but he has no memory of this at present. With the ability "Light of God," he can absorb the pain of others and heal their wounds. He's the type to put others before himself.

Yuki *(previous life)*

Luka Crosszeria
An Opast. In Infernus, as one of the Zess—the traitor clan—he was apparently treated as a slave. Despite being a Duras, he has joined up with human comrades and currently works with the Giou clan.

Sodom
Luka's retainer beast. It can also take human form.

The Zweilt

Pairs of warriors with particular abilities whose role is to protect Yuki and hunt Duras. They are reincarnated over and over to maintain their abilities and continue the war against the Duras.

Shuusei Usui
A second-year high school student. Cool, self-possessed, and a fast thinker. Has burn scars on his chest that won't fade, caused by Hotsuma. Has the special ability "Eyes of God." Alias "The One Who Sees Through All."

Hotsuma Renjou
A first-year high school student. He may be rough in speech and manner, but he loves people deep down. He once tried to kill himself. Has the special ability "Voice of God." Alias "The One Who Burns to Cinders."

Tsukumo Murasame
A first-year high school student. Kind and quiet, he has a rather gentle disposition. He is deeply devoted to his sister, Tooko. Has the special ability "Ear of God." Alias "The One Who Inquires."

Tooko Murasame
A second-year high school student, cheerful and focused on her friends. Perhaps because he resembles someone she loved in a past life, she seems to have Luka on her mind. Has the special ability "Ear of God." Alias "The One Who Inquires."

character

THE GIOU CLAN

Betrayed

Tachibana Giou
Steward of Twilight Hall. Supervises the Zweilt.

Formerly close friends

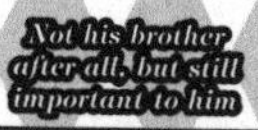

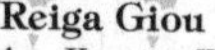

Masamune Shinmei
A second-year high school student and apprentice necromancer residing at the main residence in Kamakura.

Takashiro Giou
Commander of the Giou clan. He introduced himself as Yuki's brother, but that was a lie, as he has been alive since the "Sunset of the Underworld" a millennium ago. The most powerful of the clan, he is both a wotes and a necromancer. But might he still be hiding things from Yuki...?

Reiga Giou
As Kanata Wakamiya, he grew up with Yuki at the Morning Sun House and made it to college, but awakened as "Reiga" and became Yuki's enemy. A child of mixed blood, born to an Opast father and a Giou mother. Also a peerless necromancer.

Partners

Lia Otona
A first-year high school student and an idol singer. The lively bohemian type. Having lost her partner in the previous war against the Duras, she is now paired with Sairi.

Sairi Shinmei
A university first-year. Active in show business as an actor of some renown. A gentleman... and a ladies' man. He was overseas retrieving a Grimoire, but has returned to join up with the others. Masamune's cousin.

Partners

Senshirou Furuori
A first-year in art school. Likes cooking and taking care of people. Completely devoted to Kuroto. A "newbie" Zweilt, who has just joined for this round of the war. He has vowed to take revenge on the Opast Cadenza.

Kuroto Hourai
A first-year high school student. He grew up as a rich boy and has a self-important attitude. He was active as a professional shogi player, but quit to join the fight against the Duras. Has the special ability "Feet of God." Alias "The Swift One."

story

The Giou clan—known as the "descendants of the gods" for the special abilities possessed by many among them—has existed silently in the margins of history. Among those with such abilities, there are "necromancers," who summon and control beings known as Duras from the other world, or Infernus. It was said that these necromancers would bestow great blessings upon the people.

But a day came when the necromancer Reiga betrayed the clan. Using the Duras, he drove the Giou halfway to annihilation, then deserted them for Infernus. That was the beginning of the long war between the Giou clan, led by Takashiro, and the Duras, led by Reiga.

Time rushed onward—and now, over a thousand years later, a new battle is beginning for the Zweilt and for Yuki Giou, the boy who holds the key to a millennium-long struggle...

WE'RE FINALLY HEEERE!
AHHH! THE AIR SMELLS SO GOOD OUT HERE!
I THOUGHT IT'D BE A HASSLE TO COME ALL THE WAY TO A HOT SPRING IN THE MOUNTAINS, BUT IT SURE IS WORTH IT!
"HIDDEN SPRINGS"—IT REALLY DOES LIVE UP TO ITS NAME! ♥
AND THEY SAY THE WATER HERE MAKES YOUR SKIN SOFT AND SUPPLE.
LET'S SOAK TILL WE PRUNE! ♪
TOTALLY! BUT LET'S NOT FORGET OUR MAIN OBJECTIVE—
THE LOVE CHARM SHRIIINE! ♥♥
'COS THERE ARE TONS OF PEOPLE WHO MADE A WISH HERE AND HAD THEIR CRUSHES FALL FOR THEM, RIIIGHT!?
YEAH! I EVEN HEARD ABOUT PEOPLE FINDING THEIR SOUL MATES HERE! ♥
KYAAH! KYAAH!
OOH, WHEN SHOULD WE GOOO!?
HEY, LADIES...
IF YOU'RE GOIN' THERE TO MAKE A WISH, ISN'T THE BEST TIME FOR THAT AFTER DARK?

SO YOU CAN MAKE A WISH BY MOONLIGHT, YA KNOW?
BUT IT CAN BE SHADY GOIN' OUT AT NIGHT. BETTER STICK WITH US.
UH...NO, THANKS.
AWW, C'MON, NO NEED TO BE SHY.
YEAH. MAYBE WE'RE YOUR SOUL MATES.
SO HOW 'BOUT WE GET TO KNOW EACH OTHER?
GUI (YANK)
EEK! GO AWAY!
HOLD IT RIGHT THERE!
HUH!?
TRYING TO GET WITH GIRLS WHO AREN'T INTERESTED IS JUST PATHETIC.
HANDS OFF! NOW!

WHAT A BABE!!
OH MAN... SHE KINDA LOOKS LIKE THAT IDOL, LIA OTONASHI...
YEAHHH... DAMN, SHE'S HOT...
THANK YOUUU!
HEY, BABY, WHERE YOU FROM?
IF YOU WANNA GET TO KNOW US INSTEAD, WE'RE TOTALLY COOL WITH THAT... ♥
PA (FWIP)
C'MON, I KNOW A NICE PLACE...
GASHI (GRAB)
OH...!
HEY. YOU'VE GOT SOME NERVE GOING AFTER MY FRIEND THERE.

LOOK AT YOU, BEING ALL VIOLENT...
SEEMS YOU HAVE NO IDEA HOW TO TREAT A LADY.
!!
NO WAY! A TOTAL HOTTIE!
EVEN WITH HIS SHADES YOU CAN TELL!
HE'S A PERFECT TEN!
GOD-DAMMIT. SHE HAS A DUDE WITH HER!? CRAP ON A CRAP CRACKER!
WERE WE TALKIN' TO YOU?
GET LOST, PRICK!
FOR REAL?
YOU HAVE NO MANNERS WHATSOEVER.
OW! OW! OW! OW! OW!!
BASTARD ...!
WHAT IS GOING ON HERE?

ZA (SKSH)
OH, LUKA!
HERE WE GO AGAIN...
EEEEE!
CAN IT BE? A SECOND HELPING OF HOTNESS!!
THE GODS SMILE UPON US...!

THOSE GUYS ARE NO GOOD, LUKA.
CHASE THEM OFF.
HE CAN CHASE ME ANYWHERE...!
CHASE THEM OFF, HM...
SO I MUSTN'T HURT THEM...
じろ
JIRO (STARE)
HE'S IGNORIN' US!?
すたすたすた
SUTA (STRIDE) SUTA SUTA
WH-WHAT'S YOUR PROBLEM?
YOU WANNA GO!?
びくっ
BIKU (STARTLE)
OH!
LUKA-KU......
DOGAA (KABOOM)

PARA (CRUMBLE)
PARA
GAAAH!
THE WALL...
PARDON US!!
NICE WORK, LUKA!
AND THANKS, SAIRI.
ARE YOU OKAY, LIA?
YEP!
HE DESTROYED IT PRETTY SPECTACULARLY...
NOOO... WE'RE GOING TO HAVE TO COMPENSATE THE INN FOR IT...
LUKA-KUN, YOU IDIOT...

HEARD EVERYTHING WITH HIS EAR OF GOD.
SINCE WHEN HAVE DELINQUENTS LIKE THAT BEEN HANGING AROUND THIS PLACE?
...THOSE GUYS WHO RAN AWAY JUST NOW LOOKED LIKE TROUBLE.
THEY WERE.
...IT USED TO BE SO QUIET HERE.
REALLY?
WELL, THE LAST TIME WE WERE HERE WAS ABOUT TEN YEARS AGO.
十六夜楼
IZAYOI TOWER
HEY... WHERE'D EVERY-BODY ELSE GO?
THEY'RE ALREADY INSIDE!
YOU TOOK OFF OUT OF THE BLUE, LIA-KUN!
TACHI-BANA
UH, UMM!
ARE YOU SHOOTING A MOVIE OR SOMETHING !?
YOU WERE SO COOL!
MY, MY. IS THAT WHAT HAPPENED?

RUNNING INTO SUCH TROUBLE THE MOMENT YOU ARRIVE...
...AND THEN DESTROYING OUR OLD WALL...
WELL, THERE WAS NOTHING ELSE TO BE DONE, OF COURSE.
HOH HOH HOH!
YES...
AND WE'RE PROPERLY APOLOGIZING FOR IT!
AND WE'LL SEE TO IT THAT YOU'RE COMPENSATED!
PROPRIETRESS OF IZAYOI TOWER INN (A MEMBER OF THE GIOU CLAN)
IN FACT... THE HIDDEN SPRINGS HAVE BECOME QUITE WELL KNOWN...
...AND HAVING SO MANY GUESTS IS A BOON.
BUT WITH MORE GUESTS, WE ALSO SEE MORE MISCHIEF-MAKERS...
OH, MAKES SENSE...
BY THE WAY, MA'AM...
THOSE GIRLS WE MET WERE SAYING THERE'S A SHRINE NEARBY THAT'S GOOD LUCK FOR ROMANCE...
COULD YOU TELL US MORE?

AH, YES, THAT.
IF YOU CLIMB A BIT FARTHER UP THE MOUNTAIN, THERE IS A SHRINE, YES?
THEY SAY THAT IF YOU TIE A RED STRING TO A TREE THERE AND MAKE YOUR WISH BENEATH THE MOONLIGHT...
...YOUR BELOVED WILL RETURN YOUR FEELINGS.
AH...
SO THAT'S IT.
I WAS WONDERING WHY THERE WERE SO MANY WOMEN HERE.
CHIRA (PEEK)
チラ
CHIRA
チラ
OH YES. SINCE WORD OF THE SHRINE HAS SPREAD AROUND THE NATION...
...WE HAVE BEEN QUITE BLESSED...
DID THAT SHRINE REALLY HAVE THAT KINDA POWER?
I'VE NEVER HEARD OF IT...
I NEVER HEARD OF IT EITHER.
NOPE, ME NEITHER!

I HAD NO CHOICE, YOU UNDERSTAND. THE BENEFITS OF THE HOT SPRINGS ARE QUITE REAL. AND YET TO THE REST OF THE WORLD, WE ARE SIMPLY A REMOTE MOUNTAIN INN FAR REMOVED FROM CIVILIZATION.
HAD I BEEN UNABLE TO FIND ANOTHER SELLING POINT, I WOULD HAVE BEEN RUINED. RUINED, DO YOU HEAR ME!?
THIS IS A BUSINESS ENDEAVOR!!
SO SHE STARTED THE RUMORS HER-SELF...
GAKU
GAKU (SHAKE)
GAKU
I GET IT.
OKAY, I GET IT!!
KATA (RATTLE)
AH, AND YET...
EVEN IF IT IS TO PROTECT THE INN THAT HAS BEEN IN MY FAMILY FOR GENE-RATIONS...
...MY FOOLISHNESS MAY WELL END UP ANGERING THE MOUNTAIN GOD......
COULDN'T BREATHE...
THE MOUN-TAIN GOD?
WHAT A SINGULAR LADY...
I MUSTN'T SAY THIS TOO LOUDLY, BUT......
WHEN A COUPLE OF GUESTS WENT TO THE SHRINE AS USUAL TO MAKE THEIR WISHES...
URRGH...!!

...THEY SUDDENLY THOUGHT THEY HEARD A DEEP GROANING FROM BENEATH THE EARTH...
...AND THEN THEY WERE PURSUED BY EERIE BALLS OF LIGHT.
LATER, WHEN ONE OF THEM REALIZED SHE HAD DROPPED HER PURSE IN FRIGHT, THEY WENT BACK, TREMBLING THE WHOLE WAY...
...BUT TRY AS THEY MIGHT, THEY NEVER FOUND IT.
NOTHING
AND RECENTLY, THERE HAVE BEEN INCIDENTS LIKE THAT ONE AFTER ANOTHER.
ALL I CAN THINK IS THAT IT IS THE CURSE OF SOME MOUNTAIN GOD.
WE HAVE BEEN FRIGHTENED THAT IT MIGHT AFFECT BUSINESS, AND I REALLY WAS AT A LOSS...
BUT NOW I NEEDN'T WORRY.
ALL THE ZWEILT HAVE COME TO TAKE CARE OF THE PROBLEM FOR ME!
WHAT?!

WE'RE HERE TO TAKE CARE OF THE PROBLEM?
I AIN'T HEARD NOTHIN' LIKE THAT!
THAT SNEAKY TURD!!
HA HA HA!
I'LL LEAVE IT TO YOU!
SO THAT'S WHY HE SENT ALL OF US ALONG...
OH...
BUT TAKASHIRO-SAMA TOLD ME I MIGHT CONSULT YOU—
TAKASHIRO, HUH!?
WELL, YOU CAN COUNT ME OUT.
HE'S JUST PUSHIN' ALL THE GRUNT WORK ON US!!
WE REALLY ONLY CAME FOR SOME HOT SPRINGS R&R.
CURSE OF THE MOUNTAIN GOD OR WHATEVER...
...YOU MADE YOUR BED AND NOW YOU'LL HAVE TO LIE IN IT, I BELIEVE IS THE SAYING.
P—
PLEASE DON'T SAY SUCH THINGS!
WE'RE NOT DOIN' IT!

BELOVED ANCESTORS, OUR IZAYOI TOWER INN WAS ABANDONED BY THE ZWEILT IN A TIME OF NEED. THIS IS THE END—
QUIT THAT!
遺書
潰れます
LETTER: I AM RUINED. I HAVE NO REASON TO LIVE.
UM...COULDN'T WE AT LEAST LOOK INTO IT?
THE PROPRIETRESS REALLY IS IN A TOUGH SPOT...
WELL...
...HOW ABOUT WE SEND A TEAM TO GO HAVE A LOOK AROUND?
...I'LL GO. IF THERE ARE DAMSELS IN DISTRESS...
...I CAN'T LET IT SLIDE.
AAAH! THANK YOU, THANK YOU!
OH!
SO YOU'RE GOING, SAIRI?
THEN YOU SHOULD TAKE LIA—
HUH?
EVERYONE'S WEAK POINT: YUKI.
URGH...

THEY SAID WE GET TO PICK OUT A YUKATA!

IT'LL LOOK GREAT ON YOU TOOKO-CHAN! ♥

KYAH! KYAH!

NOT EVEN LISTENING.

......

WELL, SO MUCH FOR THAT

GUESS IT'S UP TO THE MEN.

SOOO, SHOULD THE HOTTSU AND SHUU-KUN PAIR GO...

...OR THE KURO-PII AND SEN-KUN PAIR?

IF TOOKO-KUN ISN'T GOING, TSUKKUN WILL HAVE TO STAND WATCH HERE.

TIME TO ROCK-PAPER-SCISSORS FOR IT. AND BE GOOD SPORTS NOW!

NO WAY IN HELL I'M LETTIN' YOU WIN.

LIKE-WISE.

AND HEEEERE WEEEE GOOOO!

THEY ALWAYS GET REALLY COMPETI-TIVE, DON'T THEY...?

FISTS READY!

ON THREE! ONE, TWOOO...

—SO THIS IS THE WAY UP TO THE SHRINE?

GAAAH! WE HAVE TO CLIMB ALL THESE STAIRS!?

SUCKY...

AND SAIRI ENDED UP COMIN' ALONG ANYWAY...
I'M GOING WITH YOU.
TO PROTECT THE LADIES.
YER HOPELESS, DUDE...
WHATEVS...
OH!
MAY I GO TOO?
...HEY.
WHAT? YOU'RE GOING, YUKI-KUN!?
...THEN IT'S NOT OKAY?
YOU REALLY MUSTN'T!
IF YUKI WANTS TO COME ALONG, I DON'T MIND.
......
BUT I SUPPOSE THAT MEANS HE'LL BE TAGGING ALONG TOO?
IF HE HAS SOMETHING TO SAY, HE'D BETTER SPIT IT OUT...
...AT ME, AND NO OTHER.
—

YOU CAN STAY HERE, LUKA.
YUKI...
IT'S ALL RIGHT. THERE WON'T BE ANYTHING DANGEROUS.
AND I'LL BE WITH THEM.
OKAY?
......VERY WELL.
SOMETHING DOESN'T SEEM RIGHT BETWEEN LUKA AND SAIRI-SAN...
MAYBE IF I COULD TALK TO SAIRI-SAN ABOUT IT, EVEN A LITTLE...
ALL RIGHT, WE MADE IT TO THE TOP.
BUT I DON'T SENSE ANYTHING PARTICULARLY OFF.
SAME HERE.
THERE IS A SPIRITUAL PRESENCE, THOUGH, SINCE WE'RE ON THE GROUNDS OF A SHRINE.
...ARE THOSE THE TREES YOU'RE SUPPOSED TO TIE THE RED STRING ONTO?

UGHHH...
THIS LOVEY-DOVEY STUFF IS ENOUGH TO WEIRD ME OUT...
THERE REALLY ARE A LOT OF STRINGS...
HEY, LOOK AT THIS.
CIGARETTE BUTTS.
THE QUESTION IS, WHY ARE THERE SO MANY?
—THE HELL?
WHAT KINDA ASSHOLE JUST TOSSES BUTTS ON THE GROUND AT A SHRINE!?
WHAT'S THAT GOTTA DO WITH IT?
IT MEANS WHOEVER IT WAS, WAS HERE FOR QUITE A WHILE.
OH. YEAH, YOU'RE RIGHT.
—...
WE SHOULD LOOK AROUND OVER THERE A LITTLE MORE.
COME ON, HOTSUMA.
'KAY.

—MEANWHILE...BACK AT IZAYOI TOWER—

YUKI AND SAIRI, YOU STAY HERE.
WE'LL BE BACK SOON.
ROGER.
I WONDER IF SHUUSEI-KUN SAW SOMETHING.
MAYBE.
WHATEVER IT IS, THEY'D BETTER FINISH UP SOON...
LOOKS LIKE SOME NASTY WEATHER'S ON THE WAY.
I WONDER WHAT EVERYONE'S DOING BACK AT THE INN.
WELL, I HOPE THEY'RE NOT CAUSING TOO MUCH OF A RUCKUS.
THERE'RE QUITE A FEW AMONG US WHO DON'T PLAY WELL WITH OTHERS.

MEANWHILE—KUROTO, TSUKUMO, AND SENSHIROU...
HAVING COME ALL THE WAY OUT TO A HOT SPRING...
...KUROTO AND I OUGHT TO MAKE IT SOMETHING TO REMEMBER.
KUROTO, WHERE DID YOU GO?
OHH...
THERE, OVER YONDER! KUROTO AND TSUKUMO MAKE SUCH A LOVELY PAIR...
KYUUUUUN (SWOOOON)
THEY MUST BE HEADED FOR THE CAFÉ IN THE LOBBY...
AND THE TWO OF THEM WILL EAT SWEET, TASTY TREATS TOGETHER...
BE STILL MY HEART! ♥
OH!
I KNOW!
I SHALL WATCH THEM!
THAT WILL BE SPLENDIFEROUS!
THIS IS NOT A WHOLESOME WAY OF MAKING SPECIAL MEMORIES.
CAFÉ
YOU TRANSFERRED INTO THE SAME CLASS AS YUKI AND HOTSUMA, RIGHT, KUROTO?
YEAH.
WHAT'S IT LIKE?
NOTHING SPECIAL.
AND YOU JOINED THE GO AND SHOGI CLUB, RIGHT? WITH YUKI.
HE KINDA MADE ME. I COULDN'T GET OUT OF IT.
NICE. THAT SOUNDS LIKE A LOT OF FUN...
OH...
YEAH.
I SHOULD WARN YOU ABOUT ONE THING.
IF YOU TRY TO EAT CANDY ON THE WAY TO SCHOOL, SHUUSEI WILL CONFISCATE IT.
DON'T WORRY, I WON'T.
SUCH A HEARTWARMING SCENE... ♥
...SIR? MAY I GET YOU ANYTHING?

HEY, YOU TWO, MIND IF I JOIN IN?
WHAT DO YOU WANT, SENSHIROU?
I THOUGHT MAYBE I COULD TREAT YOU TO SOME-THING...
SEN-SHIROU-SAN.
...... HURRY UP AND SIT DOWN.
THAT LOOKS TASTY... WANT TO TRY MINE TOO, KUROTO?
HM?
...WELL, IF YOU IN-SIST...
I DO! ♪
HERE YOU GO! SAY "AHHH"~!
JI (STARE)
WHAT D'YOU THINK YOU'RE DOING!?
IS TOO!
WELL, AREN'T THEY CLOSE ...
YOU'RE ALL =CHOMP=!
HUH? BUT THIS IS NO DIFFERENT FROM USUAL?
MOGU (MUNCH) MOGU
ROOM ASSIGNMENTS
KEIGETSU ROOM: • YUKI-KUN • LUKA-KUN • ME
KOKUGETSU ROOM: • SHUU-KUN • HOTTSU • TSUKKUN
SHUUGETSU ROOM: • TOOKO-KUN • LIA-KUN
RAGETSU ROOM: • RII-KUN • KURO-PII • SEN-KUN
THIS IS THE BEST SETUP TO AVOID BICKERING...
WHEW...
GO ME!

MEANWHILE—TOOKO AND LIA...

ANYWAY, FIRST THINGS FIRST...
TIME FOR A DIP! ♥
LET'S START WITH THE GRAND BATH-HOUSE! ♫

...BUT NOW THE SHRINE INVESTIGATION TEAM IS ONLY BOYS.
THEY LEFT BEFORE WE KNEW IT...
MAYBE THAT WASN'T SO NICE OF US.

IT'S FINE! YOU HAVE TO GO UP ALL THESE STEPS TO GET THERE, RIGHT?
PHYSICAL LABOR SHOULD BE LEFT TO THE MENFOLK.

ACK! LIA! DON'T TELL ME YOU GOT ME TO SNEAK AWAY WITH YOU IN THE MIDDLE OF THE DISCUS-SION ON PURPOSE!?
...... BUT OF COURSE.
THE ROLE OF MEN IS TO DO THE WORK FOR US LADIES!

MEANWHILE—TOOKO, LIA, AND LUKA...

THAT WAS A NICE SOAK.
LET'S TRY THE OPEN-AIR BATH NEXT! ♥
'KAY! ♥
FULL-ON YUKATA MODE! ♥

NOW IT REALLY FEELS LIKE WE'RE AT A HOT SPRING!
WITH THE YUKATA AND EVERY-THING! ♥
OOH, I COULD GET USED TO THIS! ♥

ZAWA (MURMUR)
SUTA (STRIDE) SUTA SUTA

ZAWA ZAWA
HE'S NOT GETTING INTO THE SPIRIT AT ALL...

SHUU-GETSU ROOM
CHANGE INTO THIS "EWEKATA," YOU SAY?
YEAH!
EVERYONE'S WEARING THEM HERE, RIGHT? SO YOU STAND OUT LIKE THAT.
IT MIGHT MAKE YUKI UNCOMFORT-ABLE, YOU KNOW?
.....
HEY, WHAT ARE YOU DOING IN THERE?
I CAN HEAR YOU OUT IN THE HALLWAY!
OH! SORRY, TACHI-BANA...
!!
......
ALL RIGHT.
IF IT'S GOING TO MAKE YUKI UNCOMFORT-ABLE...
ぬぎ
NUGI (STRIP)
EEEEEK!
OHHH, YOU'RE MAKING LUKA PUT ON A YUKATA?
THAT MIGHT JUST BE AN EXCELLENT IDEA! ☆
DON'T TAKE YOUR CLOTHES OFF HERE...
MMF!
OH!
IT'S FINE! DON'T MIND HER! YOU GO RIGHT AHEAD! ♥
YOU LOOK SO COMPLETELY OUT OF PLACE IN THAT GETUP OF YOURS, AFTER ALL.
PFFFT!
HERE, I'LL HELP YOU GET IT ON...
LOOK WHO'S TALK-ING!!
JUST HOW MANY HATS DID YOU BRING!?
WHAT!? LIA!
BUT IT'S A ONCE-IN-A-LIFETIME CHANCE!
FOR WHAT!?
AM I SUPPOSED TO TAKE THEM OFF OR NOT?
......A NICE SHOW, IF YOU KNOW WHAT I'M SAYING!
!? WHAT? I HAVE NO IDEA WHAT YOU'RE SAYING!
I DON'T WANNA BE SEEN WALKING AROUND WITH TACHIBANA...
WHAT'S UP?
OOH, YUKATA~! ♪

POTSU (PLIP)
POTSU
ZAAAA (FSSSSH)
AH! IT'S RAIN-ING?
IT'S COMING DOWN ALREADY...
QUICK, LET'S GET UNDER THAT ROOF FOR NOW.
RIGHT...
GA (TRIP)
WHOA!
DOSHA (WHAM)
WAH!!
WHAT THE—!?

ARE YOU ALL RIGHT?
OW! OW! OW!
S-SORRY...
HE'S SUCH A KLUTZ ...
MY LEG...
IF WE DON'T GET MOVING, WE'RE GONNA GET SOAKED.
HUH?
!!
THIS WAY IS FASTER.

WHOA!
AAAH!
IT'S ALL RIGHT. I WON'T DROP YOU.
I'M USED TO THIS.
TH-THAT'S NOT WHAT I...
HUH? USED TO IT??
SAAAA (FSSSH)
I WONDER IF HOTSUMA-KUN AND SHUUSEI-KUN FOUND SOMEWHERE TO TAKE COVER TOO.
PROBABLY.
BUT I'M SURE THIS IS JUST A PASSING SHOWER. IT'LL BE OVER SOON.
THERE'S CLEAR SKY OVER THAT WAY.
......YOUR LEG ALL RIGHT?
OH! YES.
GOSO (FUMBLE)

YOUR HAIR'S ALL WET.
HERE, DRY OFF, OR YOU'LL CATCH A COLD.
SAIRI-SAN...
...REALLY IS A NICE PERSON.
...OH.
THANK YOU.
...I KNEW IT.
YOU'RE TALKING TO ME NORMALLY TODAY.
HM?
DON'T I USUALLY?
WELL ...
...USUALLY I GET THE FEELING THAT YOU'RE AVOIDING ME FOR SOME REASON ......
......
I DIDN'T MEAN TO GIVE YOU THAT IMPRESSION ...

—IT'S JUST...
OH...
YEAH, I GET IT.
I...DON'T REMEMBER ANYTHING, AND... I'M A BOY THIS TIME TOO.
I'VE BEEN A LITTLE CONFUSED ABOUT...
...HOW TO ACT TOWARD YOU.
IN OUR PREVIOUS LIFE...
..."THE LIGHT OF GOD" WAS...
...A DISTANT PRESENCE, SOMEONE WE WEREN'T ALWAYS ALLOWED TO SEE OR GET CLOSE TO.
AND NOW, TO BE SO NEAR TO YOU...
...I CAN'T QUITE GET USED TO THAT FEELING.
...I DIDN'T KNOW.
THE ZWEILT WEREN'T EVEN FREE TO SEE ME BEFORE...?

THAT MUST HAVE BEEN...
...PAIN-FUL...
...WAS IT BECAUSE OF ME—?
WAS I THE REASON YOU CHOSE TO BE REBORN A MAN...?
TELL ME...
WHAT ......?
POOH!
NOW TACHIBANA'S GONE AND STOLEN LUKA!

HMPH!
I WANTED TO HELP HIM PUT ON THE YUKATAAAAA!
OH WELL... HE SAID HE'D COME GET US WHEN THEY WERE DONE.
I'LL MAKE SOME TEA.
LUKA DOESN'T EVEN LOOK VERY JAPANESE, BUT...
...SINCE IT'S HIM, I BET HE'LL BE ABLE TO PULL OFF A YUKATA JUST FINE.
...LIA?
WHA—!?
OH! SORRY!
I WAS JUST THINKING THAT YUKI AND THE OTHERS SURE ARE TAKING FOREVER...
OH!
YEAH, THEY ARE.
IT MUST BE HARD TO RELAX SINCE SAIRI-KUN ISN'T HERE, HUH...?
TH-THAT'S NOT IT!
YOU DON'T HAVE TO BE BASHFUL ABOUT IT!
THAT'S JUST HOW IT IS WITH US ZWEILT PAIRS.

....
BUT SAIRI AND I ONLY BECAME A PAIR IN THIS LIFETIME.
YOU AND THE OTHERS HAVE BEEN PAIRED UP FOR AGES. IT FEELS DIFFERENT.
KOPO (BLUB)
KOPO
...BUT THEY LET YOU PAIR WITH SAIRI-KUN...
...SO YOU MUST HAVE PASSED THE COMPATIBILITY TESTS, RIGHT?
YEAH, WE DID, BUT...
WELL...
...IT'S TRUE THAT I WAS A LITTLE SURPRISED AT FIRST...
...WHEN YOU SAID THAT YOU WANTED SAIRI-KUN AS YOUR PARTNER.
IF YOU'D HAVE ASKED ME...
...I'D HAVE SAID I THOUGHT YOU DIDN'T LIKE SAIRI-KUN VERY MUCH.
OH!
GOSH, WAS IT REALLY THAT OBVIOUS?
...YOU'RE RIGHT, I DIDN'T. I NEVER GOT ALONG WITH HIM IN OUR PREVIOUS LIVES.
HE WAS ALWAYS GOING THROUGH WOMEN LIKE TISSUES......
I TEND TO GET ALONG BETTER WITH STRAIT-LACED, HONEST TYPES, LIKE MY BIG BROTHER.

...BUT THEN...
...I FOUND OUT.
ABOUT SAIRI'S SECRET.
HIS SECRET?
YEAH.
AND THEN YOUR OPINION OF HIM DID A 180?
WHOA, WHAT THE HECK IS THIS SECRET?
HEE HEE.
THAT I CAN'T TELL EVEN YOU, TOOKO-CHAN!
AAAH! I WANNA KNOW!
...THE THING ABOUT SAIRI IS, HE'S REALLY GOOD AT HIDING HIS TRUE FEELINGS.
FOR EXAMPLE... DO YOU KNOW WHY HE WENT INTO ACTING?

UHH...
SO HE COULD ATTRACT MORE LADIES?
WRONG!
ACTUALLY, HE WOULD'VE BEEN HAPPY WITH ANY JOB HE COULD GET.
THAT'S WHAT HE SAID
HE SAW KUU-CHAN SUCCEED AS A PRO SHOGI PLAYER...
...AND DECIDED HE WANTED TO HAVE A CAREER TOO WHILE HE STILL COULD.
SO...
...HE SEARCHED HIGH AND LOW FOR A PLACE THAT WOULD HIRE A HIGH SCHOOLER...
HIS FIRST JOB WAS WAITING TABLES AT A CAFÉ.
HUH? HE REALLY DID STUFF LIKE THAT?
HE'D SURE LOOK GOOD DOING IT...
BUT THE LADIES WHO CAME TO THE CAFÉ WOULD ALL CRUSH ON HIM, YOU KNOW?
......
AND THEN, ONE DAY, A GUY CAME IN SCREAMING THAT SAIRI STOLE HIS GIRLFRIEND.
IT WAS TOTAL CHAOS.
HE PUNCHED SAIRI IN THE FACE!
NO WAY!
IN THE END, HE GOT FIRED...
...AFTER ONLY A MONTH.
THEN...
...HE TRIED LOTS OF DIFFERENT THINGS, BUT HE KEPT GETTING FIRED 'COS OF HIS ENTANGLEMENTS WITH THE LADIES.
I DID FEEL PRETTY BAD FOR HIM.
WHAT, SO LIKE HE'S CURSED WITH GIRL TROUBLE WHEREVER HE GOES...?

AT SOME POINT, AFTER IT'D HAPPENED AGAIN, AN AGENCY SCOUT DISCOVERED HIM...
OHH...
AND THEN, YOU STARTED WORKING WITH THAT SAME AGENCY, RIGHT, LIA?
BUT... I DIDN'T KNOW ANYTHING ABOUT THE STUFF WITH SAIRI. EVEN THOUGH WE'VE ALL BEEN TOGETHER SO LONG...
WELL, THAT'S JUST SAIRI FOR YOU. HE NEVER LETS ON ABOUT ANYTHING.
...BUT HE WON'T BE WORKING ANYMORE.
HE TOLD THE AGENCY THAT HE'S QUITTING.
......
...OH!
LOOK, TOOKO-CHAN...
IT'S HARD TO SEE, BUT IT'S RAINING.
SAAA (FSSSH)

...WAS IT...
...BECAUSE OF ME—?
UM...
I'M SORRY, I...
I REALLY DON'T REMEMBER ANYTHING ......
......
...OH.
RIGHT, OF COURSE NOT...
SORRY. FORGET I SAID THAT.
AH! UM!
SO YOU WERE ON A MISSION ABROAD WITH LIA ALL THAT TIME?
NO...WE WERE ONLY OVERSEAS FOR ABOUT TWO WEEKS.
BEFORE THAT, WE WERE IN KYOTO GETTING PUT THROUGH THE COMPATIBILITY TESTS REQUIRED FOR PAIRS.

KYOTO—
"WE ALSO HAVE ZWEILT ON STANDBY AT THE MAIN HOUSE IN KYOTO."
HE WAS TALKING ABOUT SAIRI-SAN AND LIA-CHAN.
—KUROTO CALLED ME AN "ORIGINAL" ZWEILT, REMEMBER?
BUT THAT'S NOT TECHNICALLY TRUE.
I BECAME A ZWEILT AT THE TIME OF THE SECOND BATTLE—
THE BATTLE THAT CAME AFTER THE SUNSET OF THE UNDER-WORLD.
BUT BACK THEN...
...THE ABILITY-BEARING BLOODLINES HADN'T YET GROWN SO DILUTED. IT WAS AN ERA WHEN THE CLAN'S POWERS STILL RAN STRONG.
AND THAT'S WHY...
...I ALSO HAVE A "SPECIAL POWER" OF ***MY OWN.***

"SPECIAL POWER"? LIKE HOW TSUKUMO-KUN IS THE EAR OF GOD, AND...
YES.
THEN...
...THAT MEANS SENSHIROU-SAN DOESN'T HAVE ONE?
THAT'S RIGHT.
AND FOR THAT REASON TOO, I'M TREATED AS AN "ORIGINAL."
THE POWER I HOLD IS...
...THE "EYE OF GOD."
TO DIFFERENTIATE IT FROM SHUUSEI'S "EYE OF GOD," IT'S OFTEN CALLED THE "EVIL EYE."
WITH ONE LOOK, I CAN PLANT A SUGGESTION IN SOMEONE'S MIND OR MANIPULATE THEIR MEMORIES.
THE EVIL EYE—
—WELL...
...AS FAR AS ABILITIES GO, I'M NO DIFFERENT, BUT I NEVER HAD A PARTNER LIKE THE OTHERS.
THAT'S THE BIGGEST DIFFERENCE BETWEEN ME AND THE "ORIGINAL" ZWEILT.
...WHY...

WHY...? BECAUSE THERE WAS NO ONE ELSE WHO COULD.
...IS THAT ALL?
...DID YOU DECIDE TO BECOME A ZWEILT?
—THE MISSION OF THE ZWEILT IS TO FIGHT ON THE FRONT LINES AGAINST TERRIBLY POWERFUL DURAS.
I GET THE FEELING THAT... YOU CAN'T BECOME ONE UNLESS YOU TRULY WANT IT WITH ALL YOUR HEART.
AND I THINK...
SEN-SHIROU-SAN...
...HAD A REASON TO BECOME ONE.
...MAYBE THE REASON THAT EVERY-ONE'S ABLE TO ACCEPT THE FATE OF ENDLESS BATTLE...
...IS 'COS THEY HAVE PARTNERS.
AN IRREPLACEABLE PRESENCE.
GETTING THROUGH THE PAIN AND SORROW TOGETHER, AS A "PAIR."

BUT YOU SAY YOU DIDN'T HAVE ONE......
...SO HOW...
...WERE YOU ABLE TO KEEP BEING A ZWEILT?
....
...WHAT ABOUT YOU?
WHY DO YOU KEEP FIGHTING THE DURAS?
FOR WHOM DO YOU FIGHT?
WHY...?
...I—
I WANT TO PROTECT ALL THE ZWEILT... TO...SAVE THEM......
AND IF THE FATE OF THE WORLD IS RESTING ON IT...
...THEN THAT'S ALL THE MORE REASON TO DO EVERYTHING I CAN—

—... BUT...
...I...
I GUESS IT'S NOT FAIR FOR ME TO KEEP QUIET ABOUT IT, SO...
...I'LL TELL YOU OF THE FINAL DAYS OF THE FORMER "LIGHT OF GOD."
YOU PROBABLY DON'T REMEMBER, BUT EVERY DAY WAS EVEN CRUELER AND MORE TERRIBLE THAN THE NEXT... MUCH MORE SO THAN YOU CAN IMAGINE.
...YOU WANT TO "SAVE" US? SAY IT WHILE YOU CAN.
WAR ISN'T PRETTY.
WHITTLING AWAY AT THE BODY...
...WEARING DOWN ON THE SOUL.
DEVOTED TO HEALING THE WOUNDS OF THE ZWEILT...
...ALWAYS TAKING OUR PAIN INTO HERSELF—
BIT BY BIT, IT BROKE US.
WHAT DO YOU THINK BECAME OF THE "LIGHT OF GOD"?

THAT TERRIBLE PAIN ACCUMULATED UNTIL SHE COULD NO LONGER BEAR IT.
IT'S SO PAINFUL.
SHE WENT MAD...
IT HURTS...
KNOWING THAT, CAN YOU STILL SAY...
...AND DIED IN AGONY.
I WANT TO BE SET FREE......
...THAT YOU WANT TO FIGHT?

UP UNTIL RECENTLY, YOU'VE BEEN LIVING YOUR LIFE AS A NORMAL PERSON...
...WITH-OUT THE MEMORY...
...OF ALL THOSE LONG YEARS LOCKED IN BATTLE SIDE BY SIDE.
AND STILL YOU CAN SAY THAT YOU'RE WILLING TO FIGHT, TO SACRIFICE YOURSELF...
...FOR THE ZWEILT—PEOPLE YOU'VE JUST MET?
—
...YES, I CAN.
...I'VE NEVER THOUGHT OF IT AS SACRIFICING MYSELF.

IF IT'S FOR YOUR SAKE AND THEIRS...
...I CAN ENDURE ANYTHING, NO MATTER HOW MUCH IT HURTS!

AN UNFLINCHING GAZE.
PLEASE, MAKE ME BELIEVE THAT.
I WANT TO HEAR YOU SAY IT.
I WANT A REAL BOND BETWEEN US.
AND THEN...
...I...
...SORRY. IT MUST'VE SOUNDED LIKE I DOUBTED YOU.

I DO BELIEVE WHAT YOU SAY.
...WON'T HESITATE...
I BELIEVE YOU......
—AND THEN...
...I...

THE RAIN...
...IT'S STOPPED.
...TO LAY DOWN MY LIFE FOR YOU.
......
MAGNIFEEK!♥
WELL, EVERYONNNNE! WHAT DO YOU THINK OF MY SARTORIAL ACUMEN?
GENIUS!!

IN A YUKATA, EVEN LUKA-KUN CAN START TO GET INTO THE INN ATMOSPHERE A LITTLE!
AND YET IT DOESN'T OCCUR TO HIM THAT HE HIMSELF IS MILES FROM FITTING IN......
THAT HAT IS GETTING ON MY NERVES.
AH!
SO! THEY SAID WE COULD HAVE THE OPEN-AIR BATH TO OURSELVES FOR AN HOUR! ♥
YAAAY! ♪
OOH, OPEN-AIR? I WANNA GO TOO!
WHAT!?
WELL THEN!
COME AND GET ME WHEN IT'S OURS, 'KAAAY? ♪
IS HE COMING IN WITH US...?
TACHIBANA, WHO DOESN'T EVEN LET US SEE HIM WITHOUT A HAT ON, LET ALONE GET INTO THE BATH WITH ANYONE ELSE!?
OOH, WE'LL GET TO FIND OUT WHAT SECRETS LURK BENEATH HIS QUESTIONABLE HEADWEAR AT LAST!
IT'LL TURN OUT THERE IS NO SECRET, MORE LIKE.
TYPICAL, WITH THAT DOOFUS.
OH, THIS WILL BE FUN, KUROTO! ♪
YOU WANTED TO KNOW WHAT WAS UNDER HIS HAT, RIGHT?
N-NOT REALLY.

WELCOME BACK.
—IS WHAT IT LOOKS LIKE, SO I THINK WE'LL BE ABLE TO TAKE CARE OF IT TONIGHT.
UNTIL THEN, PLEASE LET THE GUESTS KNOW NOT TO GO THERE AND MAKE WISHES.
YOU CAN MAKE UP A REASON.
OF COURSE. I WILL.
...HM?
WHY'S THERE SUCH A CROWD—
KYAA
KYAA
OH, YOU MUST BE HALF-JAPANESE, HUH?
WHERE ARE YOU FROM?
ARE YOU A MODEL?
THAT YUKATA LOOKS GREAT ON YOU! ♡
DO YOU MIND IF I TAKE A PICTURE?
LUKA?

YUKI!
WHAT ARE YOU UP TO?
OH, YOU'RE IN A YUKATA! ♪
GOOD, YOU'RE BACK.
LET'S GO.
HUH?
AWWW, HE'S LEAVING!
OOH, NOW WE KNOW THEIR NAMES! ♥
DIDN'T THOSE GIRLS WANT TO TALK TO YOU?
I DON'T KNOW...
THEY KEPT THEIR DISTANCE BEFORE, BUT...
...THEY ALL SWARMED AS SOON AS I CHANGED INTO THIS THING.
AND IT'S HARD TO MOVE IN. IT'S AWFUL...
I'M GOING TO CHANGE AGAIN.
OKAY...
THAT'S TOO BAD... HE LOOKS NICE IN IT...
BUT...
...THEN WHY WERE YOU HANGING AROUND THE FOYER INSTEAD OF CHANGING RIGHT AWAY?

....
...OH, I SEE!
TACHIBANA SAID...
...THAT YOU'D BE DELIGHTED TO SEE IT—
SO YOU WERE WAITING FOR ME THERE.
THANKS!
YOU DO LOOK GOOD IN A YUKATA.
IT WOULD BE A WASTE TO CHANGE.
....
YUKI......
DID SOMETHING HAPPEN?
HM?
WHY?

...NO REASON.
JUST MY IMAGINATION, I GUESS.
HEY, LUKA, ISN'T IT ABOUT TIME FOR OUR HOT SPRING DEBUT?
WHAT? IS THAT SOME SORT OF EVENT?
THAT EVENING...
SPLISH SPLASH, WHAT A GREAT BATH! ♪
LAA-LA-LA-LA-LAA! ♬
AHHH. HEAVENLY! ♥
SO THIS IS THE PUNCH LINE...

TACHIBANA... YOU'RE BEING A MEANIE, WEARING A HAT IN HERE.
EVERYONE ELSE IS NAKED SO YOU SHOULD BE TOO.
WHA !?
I CAN HAVE A HAT, CAN'T I??
BESIDES, I DESIGNED THIS HAT SPECIALLY TO WEAR TO THE HOT SPRINGS...
THAT AIN'T THE PROBLEM HERE!
BASSHA (SPLASH)
HOW'RE WE SUPPOSED TO RELAX IN A HOT SPRING WITH A WEIRDO WEARING A HAT LIKE THAT!?
GO OVER THERE WHERE NOBODY HAS TO LOOK AT YOU!
WAAAH!
HOTTSU IS A MANIAAAC!
...TOO BAD, KUROTO.
LIKE I CARE.
I KNOW BETTER THAN TO TAKE IDIOTS SERIOUSLY.
HOW DOES IT FEEL, YUKI?
YOUR FIRST TIME IN AN OPEN-AIR BATH.
PICHAN (SPLISH)
OH, THIS FEELS WONDERFUL!
...ALTHOUGH...
...IT WOULD BE NICE IF LUKA COULD COME IN TOO.
BATHING WITH A BUNCH OF OTHER PEOPLE? ABSOLUTELY NOT.
JUST AS EXPECTED...
GARA (RATTLE)
GARA
YAAAY!
BATHING UNDER THE STARS!
C'MON, TOOKO-CHAN!
YAAAH!
YAAH!
LIA, DON'T RUN! YOU'LL SLIP!

...HM?
SO THE WOMEN'S BATH IS RIGHT NEXT TO US?
URRRGH!
...CAN'T BREEE-ATHE...
WHAT, YOU FORGOT?
IF IT WASN'T FOR THAT, I'D NEVER GET INTO THIS SAUSAGEFEST OF A BATH.
I'VE BEEN WAITING, MY SWEET KITTENS! ♥
OH. IT'S SAIRI.
I GUESS THE BOYS ARE ALREADY IN.
HEEEY!
JUST AN IDEA, BUT WHAT DO YOU SAY WE GO AHEAD AND MAKE IT A MIXED BATH...?
SAIRI, YOU PERV, NO WAY ANYONE'S DOIN' THAT!
IF YOU TRY TO PEEK, YOU'RE DEAD MEAT, SAIRI-KUN!
OH, I DON'T MIND DYING, SO MAYBE I COULD POP OVER THERE...
QUIT TALKIN' STUPID!!
BASHAN (KASPLASH)
ZABAA (SPLASH)
WHAT THE HELL WAS THAT, YOU FIRE-HAPPY JACK-ASS!?
WANNA TRY SAYIN THAT AGAIN!?
IGNORE
UM...
HEY!

WHAT, ARE YOU REALLY THAT SHOCKED BY THE IDEA OF A MIXED BATH?
CUT THE CRAP.
DID YOU PANIC JUST FROM THE THOUGHT OF IT?
SO INNOCENT.
HOW 'BOUT YOU LEAVE EVERYONE OUTTA YER HORNDOG SCHEMES!!
YOU WANNA GO!?
OH!
THAT'S RIGHT!
LADIES' BATH
HYOI (POP)
HEY, GUYS...
...WHAT HAPPENED WITH TACHIBANA'S HAT?
WAAAAAH!!
HEY!
YOU GETTING A NICE VIEW THERE?
AWW, BOO. HE'S EVEN WEARING ONE IN THE BATH!?
LAAAAME!!
LIA! WHAT ARE YOU DOING!?
NO PEEKIN' INTO THE MEN'S BATH!! IDIOT!!
LIA-KUN, YOU DIRTY, DIRTY PERV!!

WHAT'S THE DEAL? YOU'RE ALL DUDES!
GET OVER IT! C'MON, THERE'S NOTHING TO BE SCARED OF!
IT'S NOT OKAY!!
LIA, GET DOWN ALREADY!
YOU'RE A CHICK! I'M SAYIN' YOU'RE THE ONE WHO'S S'POSED TO BE SHY!
WHAT IS SHE EVEN THINKING ...?
LIA...
GIRLS ARE MORE DELICATE. YOU MUSTN'T LET YOURSELF CATCH A CHILL.
GET BACK INTO THE BATH NOW, OKAY?
I WUV YOU!
SENSHIROU-SAN, YOU'RE SO SWEET.
WHAT IS WITH THAT GIRL ...?
SEN-KUN, I CAN'T BELIEVE YOU CAN KEEP SUCH A STRAIGHT FACE...
ARE YOU OKAY, YUKI?
I-I JUST FELT A LITTLE DIZZY...
THIS IS EXHAUSTING ...!!
THIS IS EXACTLY WHY I DIDN'T WANT TO COME... BUT NO, I HAD TO GO ON THIS TRIP BECAUSE EVERYONE ELSE DID...

AAAALL RIGHT!
NOW THAT WE'VE HAD OUR DINNER...
YEP.
...EVERY-ONE'S FREE UNTIL THE OPERATION COMMENCES. SO TAKE IT EASY! ♪
WE'LL MEET BACK UP AT TEN.
WHEN THE MOON RISES.
RIGHT.
ぞろ ぞろ..
ZORO (FILE) ZORO
YUKI-KUN, MAYBE YOU SHOULD...
...TAKE ANOTHER DIP IN THE MEANTIME?
......
OH. MAYBE...
...HEY.
GUYS.
ISN'T IT BOTHERING YOU?

HUH?
WHAT'S THAT, TSUKUMO-KUN?
THE MYSTERY OF TACHIBANA'S HATS.
OH... ARE WE STILL RUNNING WITH THIS GAG?
WELL, IF HE'S SO STUBBORN ABOUT IT THAT HE WON'T EVEN TAKE IT OFF IN THE BATH...
...HE MUST HAVE A GOOD REASON.
RIGHT?
ONCE, KUROTO AND YUKI-KUN TRIED TO TAKE OFF HIS HAT...
...BUT HE RAN AWAY, AND NOT AS A JOKE.
WHAT WAS THAT ABOUT...?
DOES ANYONE HERE KNOW TACHIBANA'S BACK-GROUND?
NO... WE WERE ALWAYS IN KAMAKURA...
HOW LONG HAS HE BEEN AROUND ANYWAY?
DO YOU KNOW, LUKA?
HE'S SOMEONE TAKASHIRO BROUGHT ALONG.
NOT THAT INTERESTED, ARE YOU?
↑ SEE THE ILLUSTRATION COLLECTION WITH THE DRAMA CD!

THE FIRST OF US TO MOVE INTO TWILIGHT HALL WERE HOTSUMA AND SHUUSEI.
RIGHT. AND THEY WERE ALREADY INTRODUCING HIM AS THE STEWARD THEN—
......I...
...RECALLED SOMETHING THE OTHER DAY...
I MET TACHIBANA ONCE WHEN I WAS LITTLE.
I THINK.
HUH? YOU DID?
IT MUST HAVE BEEN ...
...AT A GATHERING OF THE MAIN BRANCH OF THE FAMILY OR SOMETHING ......
MOMENTOUS REVELATION!!
IN THE HUGE GARDEN AT THE MAIN FAMILY'S MANSION ...
...I WAS PLAYING BY MYSELF, AND SOMEONE CAME UP AND TALKED TO ME—
HEY THERE.
CAN YOU TALK TO ANIMALS?

I THINK HE HAD PINK HAIR.

AND THINKING BACK NOW, I FEEL LIKE MAYBE IT WAS TACHIBANA...

PINK...

DOKI (BADUM)

ARE YOU SERI-OUS?

DOKI

A-AND HIS HAT ...?

I DON'T THINK HE WAS WEARING ONE.

SERIOUSLY —!?!

WH-WHAT WAS HE LIKE!?

W-WAS HE PARTLY BALD? OR SOME KIND OF SENSITIVE PROBLEM LIKE THAT!?

...I CAN'T REMEMBER.
GAKUU (COLLAPSE)
—THAT'S HOW IT IS...
SO, YUKI.

WILL YOU ASK TACHIBANA FOR THE TRUTH?
HUH!?
ME?
ポン
PON (PAT)
HMM...
MAYBE IF YOU REALLY BEG HIM, YUKI...
RIGHT. HE MIGHT TELL YOU.
GET GOIN' ALREADY! GO FIND OUT HIS TRUE IDENTITY!
WHAAAA!?
AFTER TSUKUMO'S STORY, NOW I REALLY WANT TO KNOW!
OR I'LL NEVER GET TO SLEEP TONIGHT...
WHAT-EVER...
桂月
KEIGETSU

AH, I SEE ......
I THOUGHT YOU MIGHT ASK ME THAT SOMETIME.
UH, UM...
IF IT'S SOMETHING SENSITIVE, I DON'T WANT TO FORCE YOU...
DUMMY! STICK IT TO HIM. THIS IS AN INTERROGATION!
HMMM... ALL RIGHT.
I SUPPOSE THERE'S NO TIME LIKE THE PRESENT.
YUKI-KUN, TO YOU I'LL REVEAL...
!!
...MY TRUE IDENTITY.

Story 41 • END

THE
BETRAYAL
KNOWS MY NAME

Story 42
TO THE GIOU HIDDEN SPRINGS
—I WON'T FORGET—

"YUKI-KUN, TO YOU I'LL REVEAL...
"...MY TRUE IDENTITY."
—I CAN NEVER LET ANYONE...
...SEE WHAT'S UNDER THE HAT.
AND WHY IS THAT, YOU ASK ...?
...BECAUSE IF ANYONE SAW MY HEAD...
...THEY WOULD KNOW THAT I AM NOT HUMAN.
GOKU (GULP)
WHAT ......?

YOU SEE, I...
...AM A DURAS.
ZAZAA (FWSSSHH)
DI—
DID HE JUST SAY...!?
SHH.
...TA—
TACHIBANA-SAN, YOU'RE ...
...A DURAS ......?

THAT'S RIGHT! HAVE I SHOCKED YOU?
AND NOT ONLY THAT, I'M AN OPAST. RANK A.
AND AN OPAST!?
IN HUSHED TONES
I CAN'T BELIEVE THIS!
B-BUT...
...YOU HAVE A PROPER NAME, A GIOU NAME......
OH, THAT. THE COMMANDER NAMED ME THAT.
<TACHIBANA> ACTUALLY WAS MY NAME AS A DURAS, THOUGH.
IT JUST HAPPENED TO SOUND LIKE A NICE JAPANESE NAME, SO...
AH! BUT DON'T GET ME WRONG. NOT ALL DURAS ARE OUT TO GET HUMANS, YOU KNOW.
IT'S JUST LIKE HOW, AMONG HUMANS, YOU HAVE GOOD GUYS AND BAD GUYS, OKAY?
AND I'M ONE OF THE "GOOD GUY" DURAS.

...WHICH ISN'T TO SAY I WAS LEADING A PARTICULARLY RESPONSIBLE LIFE OR ANYTHING.
I WAS LUCKY TO BE BORN AN OPAST.
MY POWER'S AT A RESPECTABLE LEVEL AND I DIDN'T HAVE MUCH DRIVE TO BECOME STRONGER.
"YOU'RE MY FAMILIAR," HE SAID! NEVER EVEN ASKED ME, CAN YOU BELIEVE IT?
THAT GRIMOIRE THING REALLY CAN BE A NUISANCE.
I WAS FINE WITH JUST LIVING EVERY DAY AS I PLEASED.
BUT THEN ONE DAY, I WAS *SUMMONED* BY OUR COMMANDER...
I JUST WANTED TO LIVE MY OWN EASY LITTLE LIFE. SO OF COURSE I SAID, "WHAT, SERVE AS A HUMAN'S UNDERLING? I DON'T THINK SO!"
...AND I REBELLED.
...HAVE YOU HEARD ABOUT IT? THE "REVERSAL OF RANK"—REBELLING AGAINST ONE'S FAOLAR.

RIGHT...
...IT'S WHEN THE SUMMONED DURAS TRIES TO REVERSE THE MASTER-SERVANT STANDING—
SO THEN YOU... CHALLENGED TAKASHIRO-SAN TO A FIGHT, OR...?
BUT I SHOULDN'T HAAAAVE!
YES, THAT'S CORRECT!
NOW THE COMMANDER IS QUITE STRONG, SO OF COURSE I WAS NO MATCH FOR HIM!
REALLY, I WAS COMPLETELY PULVERIZED.
...SO, I HAD NO CHOICE BUT TO OBEY HIM.
BUT WHEN I ACTUALLY SAT DOWN AND HEARD HIM OUT, THE TERMS WEREN'T SO BAD.
MY PHILOSOPHY IS TO ONLY DO THINGS THAT HAVE SOME ADVANTAGE FOR ME.
HE SAID THAT IF I SIMPLY CARRIED OUT MY DUTIES INSOFAR AS TAKING CARE OF HIS AFFAIRS THERE WOULD BE NO NEED FOR ME TO RISK MY LIFE...
...AND THAT IF THINGS GOT DANGEROUS, HE WOULD RELEASE ME, YOU SEEEE!

BESIDES!
THIS WORLD IS BRIGHT...
...AND FUN, AND FULL OF DEEELICIOUS THINGS! ♥
QUITE DIFFERENT FROM INFERNUS!
PERFECTLY COMPATIBLE WITH MEEE! ♪
COMPATIBLE......
I TOTALLY UNDERSTAND...
...WHY THERE ARE DURAS WHO COME HERE AND DON'T WANT TO GO BACK.
—SO I DECIDED TO BECOME THE COMMANDER'S ATTENDANT, AND...
...WE SIGNED A CONTRACT MAKING US MASTER AND SERVANT.
...AND THEN THERE WAS ONE STIPULATION HE ADDED. WHAT DO YOU THINK THAT WAS?
"NEVER ...
"...LIE TO ME."

...NEVER...
...LIE......
...ER, BUT WHAT DID HE—
...THAT'S IT!
WELL?
HOW WAS IT? WOULDN'T THAT BE A NEAT BACKSTORY?
...HUH?
A RATHER UNEXPECTED TURN OF EVENTS, ONE MIGHT SAY?
PFFT! PFF! PFF! PFF!
IT MIIIIGHT BE TRUE, IT MIIIIGHT NOT BE TRUE!
LIKE AN URBAN LEGEND, RIGHT? A WELL-CRAFTED STORY FOR SOMEONE LIKE ME, I SHOULD THINK~!

I MEAN...
...IF I SAID THAT I COULDN'T TAKE OFF MY HAT 'COS I HAVE THREE BALD SPOTS THE SIZE OF ¥10 COINS INDUCED BY STRESS, THAT WOULD BE TOTALLY LAME...
WHAAAT!?
"THE TRUTH IS... I WAS A DURAS ALL ALONG...!"
—NOW DOESN'T THAT DEVELOPMENT SOUND JUST LIKE IT'S OUT OF A SHOUJO MANGA? ♥
......
"MYYY, TACHIBANA-SAN ISN'T AT ALL WHAT WE THOUGHT! ♥" THE FANS WILL SAY...
...AND MY POPULARITY WILL SHOOT THROUGH THE ROOF! THAT'S HOW IT'LL GO!!
COULD BE!?
UM...
SO JUST TO CHECK...
...EVERYTHING YOU TOLD ME JUST NOW... WAS MADE UP?
...RIGHT?
...HEH.

IT'S UP TO YOU WHETHER TO BELIEVE IT OR NOT! ☆
SUPAAAN (WHAM)
WHO THE HELL'S GONNA BELIEVE THAT!?!
I'M AN IDIOT FOR LISTENING SERIOUSLY TO A STORY LIKE THAT FROM YOU!!
AAAH!
WHAT ARE YOU DOING THERE, KURO-PII?
STOP! STOP IT!!
KUROTO! CALM DOWN...
KU—
KUROTO-KUN—
10:00 PM
OOOH, WHERE DO I START ...!?
SAIRI-KUN, YOU'RE NOT EVEN A BIT DIFFERENT FROM HOW YOU LOOK ON TV! ♥
I CAN'T BELIEVE WE GET TO MEET YOU IN A PLACE LIKE THIS! WE'RE SO LUCKY! ♥

SAIRI-KUN, WE KNOW THAT YOU'RE SUPER-NICE...
...TO ALL GIRLS, BUT...
...IF YOU REALLY-REALLY HAD TO PICK, WHAT'S YOUR TYPE?
HM?
THAT'S A TOUGH QUESTION. CAN'T I LOVE ALL WOMEN?
OHH, C'MON, YOU'RE LYING!
NO, IT'S REALLY-REALLY TRUE.
A WOMAN IS BEAUTIFUL SIMPLY BY BEING A WOMAN.
OH, BUT I'M LUCKY TOO.
THIS IS A SECRET JUST BETWEEN US, ALL RIGHT? ♥
OKAY! ♥
BUT I GUESS I AM A LITTLE PARTIAL TO GIRLS WHO DON'T HAVE BOYFRIENDS... ♥
SO THERE YOU HAVE IT
KYAAAAAH!
OHH, YOU'RE TOOOO MUCH! ♥
PAKO (WHAP)
D'OW!

WHAT ARE YOU DOING OVER HERE?
IT'S TIME.
...SHUU-SEI.
SORRY. IS IT ALREADY THAT LATE?
YEAH. EVERY-ONE'S WAITING.
JIRO (GLARE)
JIRO
JIRO
YER A DEPRAVED MENACE TO SOCIETY. A SKEEZY, SHALLOW, PERPETUALLY PERVY, IMMORAL HEAP OF TRASH!!
DROP DEAD!
I'LL KILL YOU FIRST...
IDIOT... WHAT, DID YOU JUST STRING ALL THE OFFENSIVE WORDS YOU COULD THINK OF INTO A SENTENCE?
YER THE OF-FENSIVE ONE!
IT'S CALLED FAN SERVICE.
COME ON, YOU TWO!

HUH? WHAT ...?
WHY US?
PLEASE!
HOLD UP...
KYAAH! KYAAH!
WH—
WHY'S THIS HAPPENING ...?
OH, SORRY. ACTUALLY, SEE...
...I EXPLAINED THAT YOU'RE ALL COLLEAGUES OF MINE AND THAT YOUR DEBUT IS PLANNED FOR THIS YEAR.
I HAD TO COME UP WITH SOMETHING ON THE FLY...
GOD-DAMMIT, SAIRI!
QUIT PUSHIN'!
KYAAAH!
KYAAAH!
DID YOU BRING A RED RIBBON, LIA?
YEAH, GOT IT.
UGH.
SO WE'RE GONNA HAVE TO CLIMB ALL THOSE STEPS AFTER ALL.
LOOKS LIKE IT.

WHEN SHUUSEI AND THE OTHERS WENT TO INVESTIGATE, THEY FOUND TWO MORE ENTRANCES TO THE SHRINE.
THE GUYS HAVE SPLIT UP TO COVER ALL THREE WAYS IN...
...SO THOSE RATS WON'T HAVE ANYWHERE TO RUN.
• LUKA-KUN • YUKI-KUN • ME
②
WISHING TREES
③
• RII-KUN • KURO-PII • SEN-KUN
①
• HOTTSU • SHUU-KUN • TSUKKUN
STEPS
• TOOKO-K • LIA-KU
AYE-AYE!
...GOSH, THAT MAP'S SOME-THING ELSE.
TOOKO-CHAN.
OH. TSUKUMO?
THREE GUYS SIGHTED. THEY LOOK LIKE OUR RATS.
YOU'RE ON.
ROGER! HERE WE GO!
FINALLY! WE'LL CATCH WHATEVER OR WHOEVER IT IS FOR SURE!
AN ENEMY TO ALL GIRL-KIND!
Y'KNOW, WHEN WE WERE LEAVING...
...HOTSUMA LOOKED KINDA RUN DOWN OR SOME-THING...
YEAH, HE SAID THERE WERE GIRLS CHASING HIM.
IT WAS SAIRI'S FAULT.
HUH?

ARGH...
MAN, NOBODY'S HEADIN' THIS WAY.
YEAH, THE MOON'S COMIN' OUT TOO LATE. THEY'RE PROLLY ALL ASLEEP!
NAW, THERE'RE ALWAYS TWO OR THREE WHO COME 'ROUND MIDNIGHT.
HOLD ONTO YER HORSES.
SO'S EVERYTHIN' READY TO GO?
YOU BET! ♪
FIRST UP!
THE CREEPY GROANIN' WE RECORDED! WE'LL PLAY IT AT EXACTLY THE RIGHT MOMENT! ♥
HANDMADE DOODADS
VOICE RECORDER
AND THEN, THEY'LL ALL TOTALLY BE THINKING THE PLACE'S HAUNTED AND MAKE A RUN FOR IT—
NEXT!
EERIE BALLS OF LIGHT! WE'LL CHASE THE FREAKED-OUT CHICKS WITH THESE!
BUT NOT BEFORE KINDLY LEAVIN' THEIR PURSES BEHIND!

EXPLANATION
HI, EVERYONE. I'M SURE YOU'VE ALREADY FIGURED IT OUT, BUT...
WE SURE ARE LUCKY ALL THESE LADIES ARE FALLIN' FOR SUCH A DUMB TRICK! ♥
MWEH! HEH! HEH! HEH!
FOR US TO PICK UP...
...AND KEEP FOR OUR VERYYY OWN! ♥
NIYARI (SMIRK)
WALLETS
...THIS MINI-GANG'S THE REAL CAUSE BEHIND THE ALLEGED PARANORMAL ACTIVITY THAT'S BEEN TROUBLING THE INNKEEPER.
OF COURSE, IT'S NOT PARANORMAL ACTIVITY AT ALL.
THE MOANING AND THE STRANGE LIGHTS WERE BOTH CREATED BY PEOPLE.
WHAT'S UP WITH THIS DILAPIDATED GAZEBO?
IT DOESN'T SEEM LIKE ANYONE USES IT ANYMORE.
IN FACT, DURING THE DAY SHUUSEI-KUN AND COMPANY DISCOVERED THE RECORDER AND LIGHT CONTRAPTIONS HIDDEN AWAY.
AND NOW THEY'RE ABOUT TO CATCH THE CULPRITS COMPLETELY OFF GUARD!
CHIKA (STEP)
HM?
QUICK, SOME-ONE'S COMIN' UP THE STAIRS OVER THERE.
HIDE!

OVER THIS WAY, RIGHT?
YEAH.
HEYYY!
AIN'T THAT THE BABE FROM BEFORE!?
DIDN'T THINK WE'D SEE HER UP HERE...
THAT LONG-HAIRED CHICK SHE'S WITH IS BANGIN' HOT TOO.
GASASA (RUSTLE)
ALL RIGHT! LET'S GIVE 'EM A LITTLE MORE OF A SCARE THAN USUAL!
READY FOR ACTION!
TO YOUR POSITIONS, MEN!
REALLY MAKE 'EM SCREECH!
YES, SIR!
KYU (TIE)
THERE WE GO...
HUH...
...YOU'RE REALLY MAKING A WISH?
OR IS THAT JUST FOR SHOW?
HEE-HEE.
FOR GOOD MEASURE.
OOOH...
WHAT'D YOU WISH FOR, HUH?
URRR...

URRRGG
THEN THE BALLS OF LIGHT WILL BE NEXT!
I WONDER WHERE THEY'LL COME FROM...
!
THERE IT IS ALREADY! THE GROANING VOICE!
AREN'T THEY CUTE. TRYIN' TO LOOK ALL AROUND THEM LIKE THAT.
ALL RIGHT, TIME FOR THE LIGHTS!
KACHI (CLICK)
ON IT.
BOU (FLARE)
TOOKO-CHAN, THERE.
THE BALLS OF LIGHT!
HEY GUYS, OVER THERE!!
TO THINK IT WOULD BE THIS EASY...
OVER THERE?
WHERE?

ALL RIGHT!
TIME TO CATCH 'EM IN THE ACT!!
BA (LEAP)
WHAAAAAT!?
WHAT THE!!?
HOLD IT RIGHT THERE!!!
WHO ARE THESE GUYS?
HELL IF I KNOW!
WHAT'S GOING ON!?
WHATEVER, LET'S GET OUTTA HERE!!

STOP, PLEASE!!
FRIEND OF THEIRS!?
LOOKS LIKE A PUSSY.
OUTTA THE WAY!
WHO'S STOPPIN', HERE, YA THINK!?
!!
!?
SORRY...
GUH

DOSAA (THWUMP)
WHAT THE...!?
GAH!
!!
HIM TOO!?
GIRORI (FIERCE)
...YOU.
JUST COME ALONG NICELY.
ZOZOO (CHILL)
YOU'RE THE...
...FROM TODAY—!
TRAUMATIZED
ACK!
I WONDER IF IT'LL REALLY WORK...?

STAY BACK!!
BA (GRAB)
EEEEEK!
ONE STEP CLOSER, AND THIS BITCH DIES!!
!
HEH HEH...
KEEP STILL, SWEETY!
IF YOU MOVE I'LL CUT YOUR THROAT OPEN!!
WHY ARE THERE OTHER PEOPLE HERE!? DIDN'T THEY HEAR NOT TO COME TO THE SHRINE—?
THEY MIGHT BE GUESTS AT A DIFFERENT INN.
NOW WHAT?
I DUNNO...
I GUESS WE SHOULD LEAVE IT TO *HIM*.

PSSST! HEY, I THINK MAYBE YOU SHOULD LOOK OUT BEHIND YOU...
...UH?
TACHIBANA SUPER-ULTRA-MEGATON PUUUUNCH!
DOKKAAAN (KABLAMMM)
OOH.
THIS GUY'S RIDICULOUS...

JE SUIS UN CHAMPION!!
HE'S STRONG... I GUESS?
WHO IS THIS GUY...?
DOKU (GUSH)
DOKU
...AND THE MYSTERY OF THE LOVE CHARM SHRINE WAS SAFELY SOLVED.
AAAAH! THANK YOU EVER SO MUCH!!
WE DIDN'T GET TO DO ANYTHING, THOUGH.
FINE WITH ME.
—AND SO...
...THE CRIMINALS WERE APPRE-HENDED...
PEACE RE-TURNED...
...TO IZAYOI TOWER.
ZARI (KTCH)

YUKI.
LUKA.
THERE YOU ARE. I WAS LOOKING FOR YOU.
REALLY?
I WAS JUST GOING TO FIND YOU TOO!
I WANTED TO ASK YOU A FAVOR.
?

WOW!
IT LOOKS HUGE WHEN NO ONE'S IN IT.
ACTUALLY, THE OPEN-AIR BATH IS CLOSED NOW...
...BUT I ASKED THE PROPRIETRESS TO OPEN IT FOR US.
IF IT'S JUST THE TWO OF US...
...I THOUGHT, YOU MIGHT COME IN...
......
COME ON IN!
...SO THIS IS A "HOT SPRING"?
PASHA (SPLASH)
AND PEOPLE SIT IN IT AS A GROUP?
HUMAN CUSTOMS ARE ODD.
SUIII (GLIDE)
WELL...
THAT'S NOT A HUMAN CUSTOM, JUST JAPANESE... I THINK?
↑THE WATER'S SHALLOW ENOUGH TO WALK LIKE THIS

AND THIS HOT SPRING...
...HAS BEEN THE "HIDDEN SPRINGS" OF THE GIOU FOR CENTURIES.
THEY SAY ITS WATERS ARE HOLY...
...AND HOLD THE POWER TO PURIFY AND BLESS.
THESE WATERS ...?
......SO...
ピチャ
PICHA (SPLISH)
MAYBE THAT IS WHY THE AIR'S DIF-FERENT HERE.
LUKA'S BODY REALLY WOULD STAND OUT AFTER ALL.
HIS SKIN IS SO PALE, IT'S ALMOST LIKE YOU COULD SEE RIGHT THROUGH HIM.
....
BUT HIS HAIR IS JET BLACK.
AND THE EYES PEERING OUT FROM UNDER IT ARE SILVER...

JIII (STARE)
I'VE NEVER SEEN...
...SUCH A BEAUTIFUL COLOR ANYWHERE ELSE...
YUKI? IS SOMETHING WRONG?
GASP
OH— NO...
NOTHING!
I CAN'T BELIEVE I'M SO RUDE, STARING AT HIM LIKE THAT!!
OH!
I KNOW!
LET ME RINSE YOUR BACK.
ZABU (SPLASH)
THAT'S ANOTHER CUSTOM WE HAVE...
ZABU
AND I...
ZUBE (SLIP)
WHOA
YUKI!

BASSHAAAAN (KA-SPLAAASH)
....
OHHH...
NOW I'VE DONE IT...
...ARE YOU ALL RIGHT?
Y-YEAH. SORRY...
I JUST SLIPPED ON THE BOTTOM...
...I GUESS.
THAT'S THE SECOND TIME TODAY. EMBARRASS-ING...
YOU NEVER CHANGE. I CAN'T LEAVE YOU ALONE FOR A SECOND.
WHEW

...JUST LIKE IN MY PAST LIFE, YOU MEAN?
SO I WAS ALWAYS THIS CLUMSY?
OH...
NO...
I DIDN'T MEAN TO COMPARE YOU TO—
SORRY. I SHOULDN'T BRING UP THE PAST...
...YUKI?
—I...
I'M JUST A SHADOW OF MYSELF NOW, AREN'T I?
I DON'T REMEMBER HOW TO FIGHT.
I CAN'T USE MY ABILITIES AS THE LIGHT OF GOD TO THEIR FULLEST...
...WHAT ARE YOU TALKING ABOUT?
DID SOMETHING HAPPEN TODAY?

—IN THE AFTERNOON...
...SAIRI TOLD ME SOMETHING.
HOW IN THE END...
...THE LIGHT OF GOD WOULD ALWAYS GO MAD FROM THE PAIN AND DIE IN AGONY.
...!
...... IS THAT WHAT HE TOLD YOU?
YES...
...WELL, I CAN ADMIT IT TO YOU, LUKA, BUT...
...THAT DID SCARE ME A LITTLE.
I KNOW I CAN BEAR PAIN. I'M READY FOR THAT.
PASHA (SPLISH)
...BUT...
FINDING OUT IT'LL BE ENOUGH TO MAKE ME LOSE MY MIND...
—...

I GUESS THAT'S WHAT IT MEANS TO FIGHT...
BUT WHAT SURPRISED ME WAS THAT I NEVER HAD ANY HESITATION ABOUT USING MY ABILITY.
I'M STILL DETERMINED TO FIGHT.
THIS SHADOW OF MY FORMER SELF—CAN I REALLY BE ANY HELP, THE WAY I AM NOW?
WITHOUT THOSE MEMORIES...
...YOU CAN STILL SAY THAT YOU'RE WILLING TO FIGHT, TO SACRIFICE YOURSELF...
—FOR THE ZWEILT—PEOPLE YOU'VE JUST MET?
IT'S JUST...
...I WONDER IF BEING MYSELF IS ENOUGH.
AREN'T I JUST HURTING EVERYONE'S MORALE?
...WHY DID I LOSE MY MEMORIES...
...EVEN THOUGH I WANT TO PROTECT EVERYONE?
THE PAST ME MUST HAVE BEEN BETTER.
SHE WAS ABLE TO USE HER POWERS TO THEIR FULL POTENTIAL...
...AND SHE DIDN'T LET EVERYONE DOWN...
YUKI!
PASHA (SPLASH)

YOU DON'T HAVE TO COMPARE YOURSELF TO HER.
YOU'RE FINE JUST THE WAY YOU ARE.
—...
...REALLY?
REALLY.
YOU REALLY DON'T UNDER-STAND...
...HOW IMPORTANT YOU ARE.
YUKI...
...I WANT YOU TO KNOW...

WHEN I LOOK AT YOU, IT IS YOU I SEE.
RIGHT NOW.
I'M SEEING YOU. AND THEY DO TOO...
FOR US...
...YOUR PRES-ENCE...

...IS JOY ITSELF.
AND I'M THE ONE WHO'S ALWAYS THINKING...
...THAT I DON'T WANT TO LET YOU DOWN—...
...OH...
THANKS, LUKA.
...I'M SORRY.
UGH... THIS IS WHAT I HATE ABOUT MYSELF.
I'M SO NEGA-TIVE...
REALLY? ISN'T THAT JUST CALLED MODESTY?
I'M THE WORST
I MUST REFLECT ON MY FAULTS...
NO, IT'S SELF-DEPRECA-TION.
CHUCKLE
OOH... HNNGH...
—...
COME TO THINK OF IT...
...LUKA HAS NEVER ONCE TOLD ME...

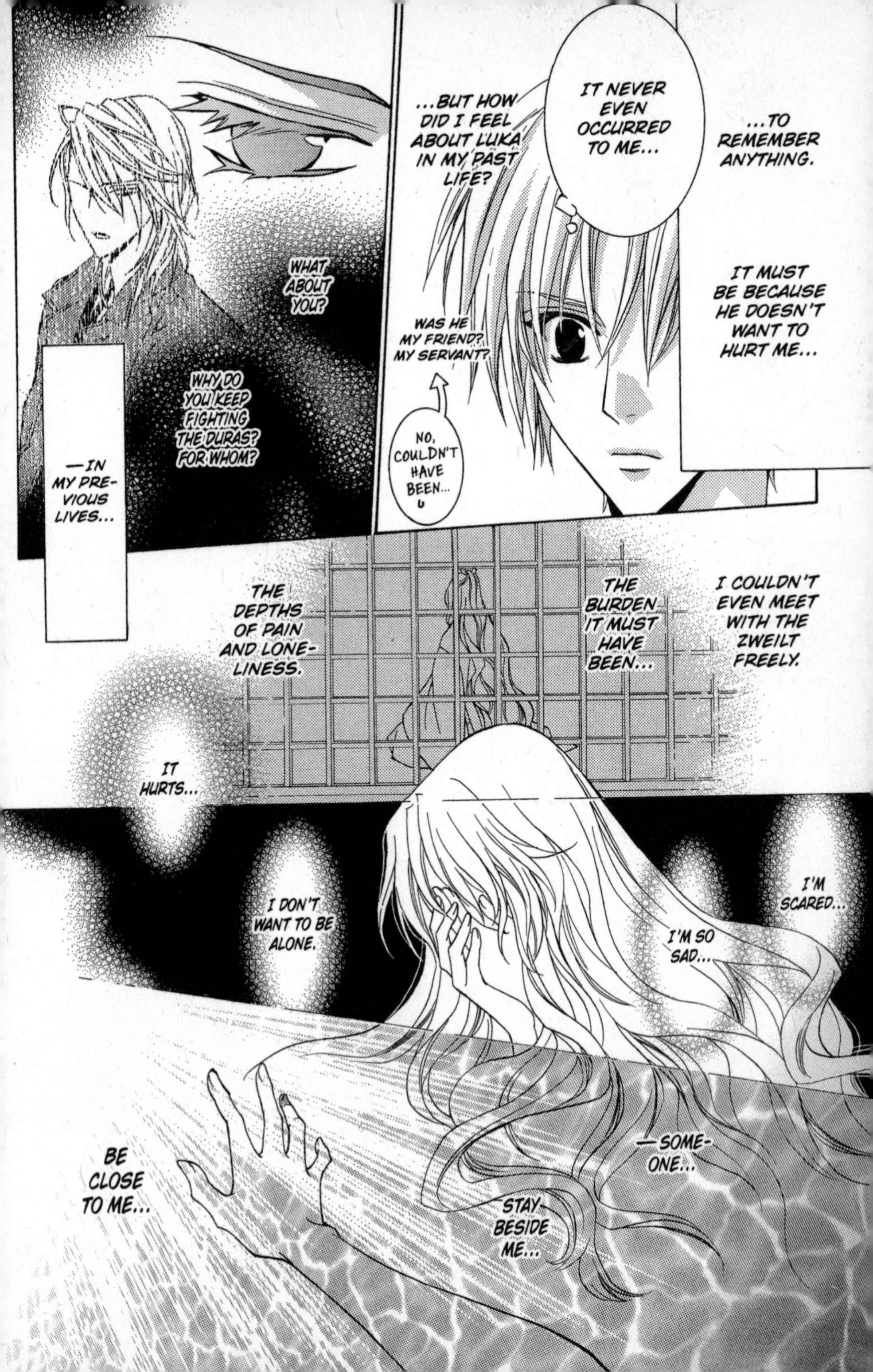
IT NEVER EVEN OCCURRED TO ME...
...TO REMEMBER ANYTHING.
IT MUST BE BECAUSE HE DOESN'T WANT TO HURT ME...
...BUT HOW DID I FEEL ABOUT LUKA IN MY PAST LIFE?
WAS HE MY FRIEND? MY SERVANT?
NO, COULDN'T HAVE BEEN...
WHAT ABOUT YOU?
WHY DO YOU KEEP FIGHTING THE DURAS? FOR WHOM?
—IN MY PREVIOUS LIVES...
I COULDN'T EVEN MEET WITH THE ZWEILT FREELY.
THE BURDEN IT MUST HAVE BEEN...
THE DEPTHS OF PAIN AND LONELINESS.
IT HURTS...
I'M SCARED...
I'M SO SAD...
I DON'T WANT TO BE ALONE.
—SOMEONE...
STAY BESIDE ME...
BE CLOSE TO ME...

SOMEONE...
......THAT'S IT.
THAT'S WHAT I'LL DO.
HM?
NOTHING.
JUST TALKING TO MYSELF.
THE MOON SINKS.
SLEEPING LIKE A ROCK
THE SUN RISES.
AND A NEW DAY BEGINS—

CHUN (CHIRP)
CHUN
I'M SORRY TO WAKE YOU ALL SO EARLY...
AND TO MAKE YOU LEAVE BY THE BACK WAY LIKE THIS...
DOSU (JAB)
SORRY ABOUT THAT.
IT WOULD BE A PROBLEM IF THE LADIES MADE A FUSS OVER SEEING ME LEAVE...
OUCH
OH, NOT AT ALL, IT'S REALLY RII-KUN'S FAULT.
NOW THAT THE WORD OF HIS CELEBRITY STATUS IS OUT WE HAVE TO TAKE MEASURES TO AVOID TROUBLE...
TROUBLE LIKE FAN-GIRLS AMBUSHING OR FOLLOWING US.
AND IT LOOKS LIKE LUKA-KUN GAINED SOME FANS OF HIS OWN...
THE CAR CAN'T COME OVER THIS WAY...
...SO IT'S WAITING IN A LOT JUST A FEW MINUTES' WALK FROM HERE.
YOUR LUGGAGE IS ALREADY THERE.
THANK YOU SO MUCH.
YOU'VE BEEN SO KIND TO US.
OH, NO, THANK YOU.
PLEASE DO COME HERE TO RELAX AGAIN.
FOR ALL OF YOU, THE LIGHTS AT IZAYOI TOWER...
...WILL ALWAYS BE ON.

THANKS.
WE WILL—
—SO, THE FATE OF THE WORLD...
...RESTS ON THEM...
MY PREDECES-SOR WAS ALWAYS TELLING ME OF IT.
WHEN HE WANTED TO SHOW HIS APPRECIATION OF THEIR HARD-SHIPS ON THE BATTLEFIELD...
...TAKASHIRO-SAMA WOULD ALWAYS SEND THEM HERE, TO IZAYOI TOWER...
I'M SURE...
...THAT WAS THE CASE THIS TIME TOO—...

HIS APPRECIATION...
HM. I THINK YOU'RE RIGHT.
I'M GLAD THAT EVERYONE COULD COME.
...THEY'LL BE ABLE TO LOOK BACK ON IT FONDLY.
WELL...
I'D BETTER GET GOING TOO.
I PRAY FOR YOUR VICTORY.
AHH!
THE MORNING AIR SURE DOES FEEL NICE. ♫
I WAS SO UPSET THAT BECAUSE OF SAIRI WE HAD TO GET UP EARLY AND GO FOR A HIKE...
...BUT I GUESS IT'S NOT SO BAD♪
YEAH!
MY APOLOGIES TO THE HIGH-BORN LADIES WITH DELICATE CONSTITUTIONS.

SO OUR HOT SPRINGS TRIP IS OVER ALREADY.
NOW WE'LL GO BACK TO TWILIGHT HALL...
AND THEN......
...YUKI.
ARE YOU ALL RIGHT?

OH......
LUKA..
YUKI-CHAN?
...OH......
UM...
ER_
SORRY.
I'M......
I GUESS I'M...
...A LITTLE SAD.
IT WAS SO MUCH FUN...
...GOING ON A TRIP WITH EVERYONE.
REALLY GREAT...
I WAS JUST FEELING LIKE I DON'T WANT IT TO END...
LIKE IT WOULD BE NICE...

ZA (TMP)
KUSHA (RUFFLE)
...AW, DON'T MAKE THAT FACE.
...IF WE...
...COULD STAY LIKE THAT FOR-EVER—
WE CAN COME BACK, Y'KNOW!
YEAH! WE WILL!
LET'S COME AGAIN, ALL OF US!
WHENEVER YOU WANT, YUKI!
YEAH.

AND NEXT TIME...
...I'LL MAKE SOME BENTO BOXES.
THAT'D BE NICE.
LONG AS YOU DON'T FORGET THE SWEETS.

OKAY......!
—AND I...
...WON'T FORGET.
♪

THIS TIME WE SPENT...

...UNDER THE SUNLIGHT, ENFOLDED IN KINDNESS.

ALL OF US...

...SMILING AT ONE ANOTHER.

...I WON'T FORGET.

...EVER.

BUT...

...THAT WAS THE FIRST AND LAST TIME...

...THAT ALL OF US WENT ON A TRIP TO-GETH-ER.

Story 42 · END

THE
BETRAYAL
KNOWS MY NAME

Story 43
—HAVE YOU...
...EVER WISHED TO KILL ANOTHER PERSON?
YES...
I HAVE.

Story 43
PROLOGUE

THE
BETRAYAL
KNOWS MY NAME

PU (BEEP)
PUUUU
SENSHIROU!
SORRY. DID YOU WAIT LONG?
NO, I JUST GOT HERE.
WHEW
REALLY? THAT'S GOOD TO HEAR.

I HAVEN'T SEEN YOU IN A WHILE.
NIKO (SMILE)
HOW HAVE YOU BEEN?
F-FINE! SAME AS USUAL!
KURU (WHIRL)
LE-
LET'S GO.
OKAY.
YOU WANTED TO FIND A BIRTHDAY PRESENT FOR IBUKI-SAN, RIGHT?
GOT ANYTHING IN MIND?
SORRY TO MAKE YOU MEET UP WITH ME IN THE MIDDLE OF A WEEKDAY LIKE THIS.
AREN'T YOU BUSY?
NO, IT'S FINE.
OH— NOT YET. I WAS HOPING TO LOOK AROUND.
BUT WHAT ABOUT YOUR CLASSES?
I DON'T HAVE ANY NOW.

HUH? IT'S STILL SUMMER VACATION?
IT IS... BUT...
I GUESS I DIDN'T TELL YOU.
I AM TAKING LEAVE.
...OH. I SEE.
YEAH. I WOULD HAVE HAD TO SOONER OR LATER.
SO I THOUGHT I'D JUST LEAVE AT THE END OF THE TERM.
I GET A LITTLE ILLUSTRATION AND DESIGN WORK TO KEEP ME BUSY, ANYWAY.
....
BUT I AM JUST ON LEAVE. I HAVEN'T DROPPED OUT.

I FULLY INTEND TO GO BACK.
...RIGHT.
SO I HAVE ALL THE TIME IN THE WORLD TO SPEND WITH YOU TODAY, TSUBAKI.
LET'S PICK OUT A PRESENT.
OH, REALLY, NOW?
YOU MIGHT SAY THAT, BUT YOU WON'T BE ABLE TO GET KUROTO OUT OF YOUR HEAD!
AHAHA!
BUT WHEN IT'S TIME FOR HIM TO COME HOME YOU'LL GET ALL DISTRACTED AND ANTSY, WON'T YOU.
HE MUST BE IN SCHOOL NOW.
WELL, I GUESS SO...
AT LEAST TRY TO DENY IT...
BUT HE'S GOT EXTRACURRICULAR ACTIVITIES, SO HE WON'T BE HOME UNTIL LATE.
EXTRA-CURRICULAR ACTIVITIES? SERIOUSLY, KUROTO!?
WOOOOW. SO HE REALLY IS A HIGH SCHOOL STUDENT NOW.
YOU'RE TALKING LIKE HE'S AN ALIEN OR SOMETHING...

SO WHAT CLUB IS HE IN?
THE GO AND SHOGI CLUB.
SAME AS YUKI.
KACHA (KTAK)
KACHA

WHOA!!
OH, THIS IS NO GOOD. I'M TWO PIECES SHORT.
HE'S PLAYING FOUR GAMES AT ONCE AND WINNING ALL OF 'EM!
HOURAI-KUN SURE IS SOME-THING!
JARA (CLACK)
ジャラ
YEAH, IT IS!
JUST BEING ABLE TO KEEP TRACK OF FOUR DIFFERENT GAMES AT THE SAME TIME IS, LIKE, SUPERHUMAN!
IT'S NOT THAT IMPRESSIVE.
A GOD WALKS AMONG US!
QUIT YOUR BROWN-NOSING! NOW, LET'S STUDY THE MOVES IN THIS GAME FROM THE BEGINNING.
KUROTO-KUN LOOKS LIKE HE'S HAVING FUN.
—SINCE THEN...
...LIKE TAKASHIRO-SAN PRE-DICTED, THERE HAVEN'T BEEN ANY MAJOR BATTLES.
THOUGH WE'VE HAD TO TAKE CARE OF SOME LOW-LEVEL DURAS.
NOW WE'VE STARTED THE SECOND SEMESTER.

DURING SUMMER VACATION THERE ARE INTER-SCHOLASTIC EVENTS, SO WE SPENT OUR DAYS IN OUR CLUB ACTIVITIES.
AND IT WENT BY BEFORE WE COULD BLINK.
TENNIS TEAM
ARCHERY TEAM
PARTICIPATING IN THE GO TOURNAMENT
NOT PARTICIPATING IN TOURNAMENT, BUT COACHING
EVERYONE WAS SO EXCITED WHEN I BROUGHT KUROTO-KUN TO THE GO AND SHOGI CLUB.
AND THANKS TO HIS COACHING...
...THE MARI IZUMI ACADEMY GO AND SHOGI CLUB HAS ACQUITTED ITSELF VERY WELL AT ALL THE TOURNAMENTS THIS YEAR.
AHEM
—BY THE WAY, HOURAI-KUN...
IT'S ABOUT TIME WE TALKED ABOUT COACHING IN SHOGI AS WELL...
HIS SENIORS IN THE CLUB
ジャラ JARA
ジャラ JARA
I TOLD YOU, I DON'T PLAY SHOGI.
WHY NOOOT!?
A PRO SHOGI PLAYER RIGHT IN FRONT OF US AND HE WON'T EVEN PLAY! IT'S TOO MUCH TO BEAR!!
WHAT A WASTE!!
I'M NOT PRO ANYMORE!!

IF YOU'RE NO LONGER A PRO, ALL THE MORE REASON TO PLAY!
WHY WON'T YOU PLAY ANYMORE!?
DON'T LET ALL YOUR SKILL GO DOWN THE TUBES!
"WHY" DOESN'T MATTER! I WON'T!
KUROTO DOES SEEM TO BE HAVING FUN.
BUT I WANNA PLAY WITH YOUUU!
I'M GLAD I INVITED HIM TO JOIN THE CLUB.
HE'S SO POPULAR!
WHAAAAAT!?
OH, BUT HE DOES PLAY WITH ME.
NO FAIR!!
BRAG-GING.
UGH, SHUT UP.
LATELY, EVERY DAY IS THIS LIVELY...
IT'S A LITTLE FUNNY, BUT...
KARAAAN (DOOONG)
WELL, TIME'S UP. LET'S GO, YUKI.
YOU'RE LEAVING ALREADY?
GATA (TUNK)
YEAH.
WE CAN GO MEET UP WITH LIA-CHAN AND THE OTHERS.
LIA-CHAN TRANSFERRED IN TO MARI IZUMI ACADEMY AS WELL.
I WANTED TO WEAR...
...THE SAME UNIFORM AS YOU GUYS!

ACTUALLY TOOKO-CHAN SAID SHE WANTED TO HELP TSUKUMO-KUN WITH THE STUFF FOR THE INTER-SCHOLASTIC EVENTS...
...AND THE TWO OF THEM BECAME MANAGERS FOR THE BOYS' TENNIS TEAM.
THANKS FOR COMING TO PRACTICE, EVERYONE! ♥
HERE YOU GO, GUYS, DRINK UP!
ALL RIGHT! ♥
......
DON'T MIND IF I DO!
THANKS!
MAN, IT'S A DREAM COME TRUE.
WOO-
HOO!
SHE MIGHT'VE QUIT BUT IT'S STILL AN IDOL TAKING CARE OF US... ♥
YEAH. EVERY DAY'S COMIN' UP ROSES...!!

TODAY'S THE DAY. I'M GONNA SEE IF I CAN AT LEAST GET HER E-MAIL ADDRESS.
I'LL FOLLOW HER OUT AND THEN...
GACHA (OPEN)
TSUKUMO.
TOOKO, LIA...
ARE YOU DONE YET?
HI!
AW, NOT AGAIN...!!
WE'LL BE READY SOON.
OKAY!
FOR THE FORMER IDOL SINGER LIA-CHAN...
...THERE'S BEEN AN EFFORT ON THE SCHOOL'S PART TO LET HER ENJOY A NORMAL, CALM STUDENT LIFE...
GIRO (GLARE)
GIRO
GIRO
IF LOOKS COULD KILL...
...BUT SHE STILL GETS FOLLOWED AROUND ALL THE TIME.
SO WE ALL WALK HER HOME AS MUCH AS POSSIBLE.
THE STALKERS ARE A REAL PAIN.
WHAT A LOT OF TROUBLE.
BUT WE CAN'T LET TSUKUMO-KUN BODYGUARD HER ALL BY HIMSELF.
AND HIS RELATIONSHIP WITH HIS SENIORS ON THE TENNIS TEAM WOULD GET COMPLICATED...
SO, HERE WE ARE NOW...

...LEADING OUR NORMAL STUDENT LIVES—
SO COMMONPLACE, AND PRECIOUS.
WHERE'S HOTSUMA?
OH—
HE SAID HE WAS GOING SHOPPING WITH SHUUSEI-KUN.
FOR THE CLASS TRIP.
OH, YEAH...
I NEED TO DO THAT SOON TOO.
OOH, SECOND YEAR SOUNDS EXCITING!
YOU'RE LEAVING NEXT WEEK, RIGHT?
KATSU (KTCH)
YEAH. IT'S A WEEK-LONG TRIP.
WE GET TO SEE KYOTO AND NARA, AND THEN WE GO TO SHIKOKU—
KATSU
KATSU
THEN YAMAGUCHI AND HIROSHIMA.
OH, THAT DOES SOUND NICE.
BUT, BUT, WE COULD CHOOSE TO GO ON AN OVERSEAS TRIP TOO!
BUT NO, TAKASHIRO-SAMA SAID...
...JUST IN CASE, WE HAD TO PICK THE DOMESTIC ONE—
ZAWA (CHATTER)

...HUH?
WHAT'S HE...?
KATSU (KTCH)
KATSU

...YUKI...
I'M HERE TO GET YOU.
RIGHT.
THANKS, LUKA.
ACTUALLY, I'M GOING TO SEE KAYAKO-SAN NOW.
DON'T WORRY, YOU CAN ALL GO HOME WITHOUT ME.
HUH... WHAT?
IS SOMETHING GOING ON?
OH... YOUR AUNT KAYAKO?
MASAMUNE-KUN'S MOTHER, RIGHT?
SHE'S NOT WELL AGAIN.
MASAMUNE-KUN IS WORRIED...
SO HE ASKED ME TO GO CHECK ON HER FOR HIM.
AND LUKA'S GOING WITH ME.
YOU'RE GOING TO VISIT HER? WE SHOULD GO TOO!
IT'S NOT TOO FAR FROM HERE, IS IT?
WHO'S THAAAT~!?
UH... WHERE WAS HER PLACE AGAIN?
OH...THE CLOSEST STATION IS UENO.

THEN IT'S REALLY CLOSE BY TRAIN!
BUT... WON'T THAT BE TOO MANY PEOPLE FOR HER?
I WON'T GO.
OH......
IT WAS MY FATHER'S FAULT...
...THAT GRANDFATHER GARAN DIED.
IF I WENT...
...I'D ONLY MAKE HER UPSET.
RIGHT. KUROTO-KUN'S MASTER...
SO, YOU CAN ALL GO.
I'LL GO HOME BY MYSELF.
SURU (TOUCH)
DON'T SAY SUCH LONELY-SOUNDING THINGS, KUU-CHAN.
WHA ...!
I'LL GO HOME WITH YOU. ♥

LET ME GO, YOU IDIOT...!
WELL, LET HER KNOW KUU-CHAN AND I WISH HER WELL! ♪
SURE.
...KUROTO SEEMS SO INCONSIDERATE...
...BUT AT TIMES LIKE THIS HE REALLY IS THOUGHTFUL...
I GUESS HE'S SENSITIVE LIKE THAT.
HE'S SUCH A GREAT PERSON...
KUROTO-KUN!
PINPOOON (DING-DONG)
301
Shinmei
GACHA (OPEN)
YES, WHO IS IT...?
HUH...!?
SAIRI-KUN? WHY ARE YOU HERE!?

パタパタ
PATA (PATTER) PATA
YUKI-SAMA?
OH, YOU'RE ALL HERE...
HELLO.
SORRY IT'S BEEN SO LONG, MA'AM.
UM— MASAMUNE-KUN SAID YOU WEREN'T FEELING WELL...
HOW ARE YOU?
OH... YOU CAME ALL THE WAY HERE JUST BECAUSE OF THAT?
YOU REALLY DIDN'T HAVE TO...
I REALLY DO APPRECIATE IT.
THIS IS KAYAKO SHINMEI, MASAMUNE-KUN'S MOTHER.
AFTER HIS FATHER PASSED AWAY, SHE RAISED MASAMUNE-KUN AND HIS LITTLE BROTHER BY HERSELF.
BUT KNOWING THAT THE LIGHT OF GOD (THAT IS, ME) WAS ALIVE GAVE HER HOPE AND COURAGE...
...AND MASAMUNE-KUN SAID THAT IF I WENT TO SEE HER SHE MIGHT FEEL BETTER.
SO SINCE THEN, I'VE COME TO VISIT KAYAKO-SAN A FEW TIMES, SINCE HER STRENGTH IS FAILING.

SHE'S THIN... SHE LOOKS SO FRAGILE ...
AND IT WAS BE-CAUSE—
OH! FIRST, WOULD YOU MIND PAYING YOUR RESPECTS TO YAMATO-KUN?
US TOO, MA'AM?
YES. THANK YOU.
AND THIS SPRING SHE COLLAPSED AND WAS HOSPITAL-IZED.
YAMATO SHINMEI-KUN.
MASAMUNE-KUN'S LITTLE BROTHER......
IN APRIL, YAMATO-KUN DIED IN A TERRIBLE ACCIDENT.
HE WAS FOOLING AROUND WITH FRIENDS AND HE FELL OUT OF THE FOURTH-STORY WINDOW OF HIS SCHOOL BUILDING.

HE WAS ONLY IN HIS THIRD YEAR OF MIDDLE SCHOOL, WASN'T HE...
M-HM...
AND KAYAKO-SAN TOOK A SHOCK AND COLLAPSED.
...MASA-MUNE-KUN TOO...
...MUST BE HURTING TERRIBLY.
BUT HE'S ALWAYS SO CHEERFUL WHEN I SEE HIM—
I NEVER SUSPECTED.
MASAMUNE REALLY MADE TOO MUCH OF A FUSS.
SAIRI-KUN WAS WORRIED TOO, AND HE CAME TO SEE ME...
WELL, I RECEIVED THIS TERRIBLY UPSET-SOUND-ING PHONE CALL FROM MY COUSIN...
...TELLING ME THAT YOU'RE ILL, KAYAKO-SAN...
HOW COULD I NOT COME RUNNING?

YOU DO HAVE SOME COLOR IN YOUR FACE. I'M NOT SO WORRIED NOW.
CHUCKLE
WELL, THANK YOU.
BUT I'M QUITE ALL RIGHT NOW.
IT HASN'T BEEN SO BAD LATELY...
I FEEL BETTER SINCE YUKI-SAMA HAS BEEN COMING TO VISIT.
—SAIRI, WHAT ARE YOU DOING OVER HERE?
JUST WHAT IT LOOKS LIKE. I'M MAKING DINNER FOR KAYAKO-SAN.
GUTSU (BUBBLE)
ぐつ
ぐつ
GUTSU
WHAAAA?
SAIRI-KUN, YOU CAN COOK?
THAT'S HOT!!
YES, I CAN. USUALLY ONLY FOR MYSELF, THOUGH.
SINCE MY MOTHER WASN'T AROUND.
...SHE WASN'T?
NOPE... MY FATHER MUST HAVE HAD TEN GIRLFRIENDS. SO SHE LEFT.
I DON'T EVEN REMEMBER HER FACE...
...WELL, I DIDN'T SEE MUCH OF MY FATHER, EITHER.

...THAT MUST HAVE BEEN HARD FOR YOU, SAIRI-KUN.
MY LATE HUSBAND'S ELDER BROTHER IS HIS FATHER.
OUR FAMILY DIDN'T HAVE MUCH OF A RELATIONSHIP WITH YOURS...
THAT MUST HAVE BEEN WHY.
WELL, ALL OF YOU HAVE HAD MORE THAN YOUR SHARE OF HARD-SHIPS.
YOU BEAR A CRUEL FATE.
SUCH TRIALS AND TRIBULA-TIONS YOU ENDURE...
YES, YOU TOO—
...LUKA-SAN... WASN'T IT?

I HEARD RUMORS ABOUT YOU, BUT I NEVER THOUGHT I WOULD GET TO MEET YOU.

THE OPAST WHO DEFECTED FROM THE ENEMY AND JOINED OUR SIDE—

THAT MUST HAVE BEEN HARD AS WELL.

A DIFFICULT CHOICE TO MAKE...

AND THERE ARE THOSE AMONG OUR CLAN WHO SPEAK ILL OF YOU.

BUT, PLEASE...

YOU, AND ALL OF THE ZWEILT...

...PLEASE, PROTECT YUKI-SAMA.

YES...
I INTEND TO.
......
OH, THAT'S GOOD.
YOU AREN'T SCARED OF LUKA.
WHY WOULD I BE?
I DON'T SENSE ANY-THING FROM HIM TO MAKE ME SHRINK IN FEAR.
SEE?
......

SOMETIMES, I WONDER...
WHAT EXACTLY CAN BE SO DIFFERENT ABOUT HUMANS AND DURAS?
WHICH ARE TRULY THE MORE FRIGHT-ENING—?
SORRY ABOUT THAT, HOTSUMA.
I REALLY DRAGGED YOU ALL OVER THE PLACE.
WHAT-EVER.
YOU SURE YOU DIDN'T FORGET ANYTHING?

—...

HEY, LIGHTEN UP.

HUH!?
WHAT'S THAT S'POSED TO MEAN?

I'M SAYING YOU'RE IN A FOUL MOOD.

PFF..
I AIN'T IN NO FOUL MOOD!

YEAH, RIGHT.
IT'S WRITTEN ALL OVER YOUR FACE, YOU DON'T WANT ME TO GO ON THE TRIP.

GU (GRIT)

I'LL BRING YOU LOTS OF SOUVENIRS...
DON'T TREAT ME LIKE A BABY!
—I DON'T GET WHAT TAKASHIRO'S THINKIN'...
DOES HE USUALLY GIVE US THE OKAY TO GO ON CLASS TRIPS...?
WHY NOT? THERE'S NO SIGN THAT REIGA IS MAKING ANY MOVES.
STILL!
WHAT IF HE ATTACKED OUT OF NOWHERE?
WHAT WOULD YOU DO WITHOUT ME THERE!?
...YEAH, IT'S NOT COMPLETELY IMPOSSIBLE—BUT YOU GET IT, RIGHT?
IF YOU LIVE IN FEAR, ALWAYS THINKING ABOUT "WHAT IF," YOU'LL BREAK DOWN.
YEAH, WE HAVE TO BE READY, BUT WE HAVE TO BE DESENSITIZED TO IT TOO. *ESPECIALLY* US.
IF EVERYONE JUST WENT AROUND THINKING ABOUT HOW THEY MIGHT DIE, NOBODY WOULD EVER GET ON AN AIRPLANE, OR EVEN SMOKE A CIGARETTE.
NOBODY WOULD BE ABLE TO DO ANYTHING.
......
...I GET WHAT YOU'RE TRYIN' TO SAY 'N' ALL.
THAT'S THE WAY IT'S ALWAYS BEEN—
...BUT STILL...

IT'S JUST...
RIGHT NOW, FOR SOME REASON... I JUST DON'T WANNA BE AWAY FROM YOU......
"DON'T LEAVE ME HERE.
DON'T GO ANYWHERE."
YOUR WHOLE BODY IS YELLING IT.
YOU DON'T EVEN TRY TO HIDE IT.
AND THAT'S WHAT...
—"RIGHT NOW, FOR SOME REASON," YOU SAY...
ACTING ON YOUR INSTINCTS LIKE ALWAYS.
HUH?
WHEN WE WERE LITTLE—

I'D GO OVER TO YOUR HOUSE, RIGHT?
AND WHEN IT GOT LATE AND WE KNEW I'D HAVE TO GO HOME SOON, YOU'D GET QUIETER AND QUIETER.
IN THE END YOU'D SHUT ME IN YOUR ROOM.
—... HUNH?
I SERIOUSLY DID THAT...?
EVERY-THING YOU'RE FEELING SHOWS IN YOUR FACE.
YOU ACT WITHOUT THINKING.
YOU REALLY ARE HONEST.
OR UNCOM-PLICATED, OR SOMETHING... SO MUCH THAT I'M JEALOUS.
YOU POSSESS WHAT I LACK.
OH, THAT'S NICE.
MAKIN' ME SOUND LIKE SOME STUPID KID WHO'S ALL SIMPLE AND EASY TO READ.
THAT'S NOT IT AT ALL.
IT'S A COMPLI-MENT.
BECAUSE THAT'S—

—WHAT I LOVE ABOUT YOU.
......
YOU...

...DON'T SAY STUFF LIKE THAT!!
DON'T JUST BUST OUT WITH STUFF YOU NEVER SAY!
GONNA MAKE ME THINK IT'S THE END OF DAYS OR SOME-THING!!
...I MEAN, NOW I'M WORRYIN'.
LIKE MAYBE YOU'LL LEAVE ME WITH THIS ONE LINE I NEVER HEARD BEFORE...
...AND THEN DISAPPEAR NEVER TO BE HEARD FROM AGAIN!
...THAT'S A NASTY WAY TO PUT IT.
END OF DAYS, HUH...
...THAT AIN'T LIKE YOU AT ALL...!
WHY CAN'T YOU JUST MAKE THAT SULLEN FACE...
...AND YELL AT ME FOR BEIN' A BRAT LIKE USUAL?
YOU WANT ME TO YELL AT YOU?
NO!
I'M SAYIN' YOU'RE BEIN' WEIRD!
YOU'RE FREAKIN' ME OUT!

—"DISAP-PEAR"... HUH?
DON'T WORRY... WELL, IT'S NO USE SAYING THAT, IS IT?
SINCE I'M THE ONE WHO DECIDED TO GO SOMEWHERE WITHOUT YOU......
—...
HOTSUMA— I'LL JUST SAY THIS WHILE I CAN.
THAT, RIGHT THERE!
ALL THIS "WHILE I CAN"—
GU (GRAB)
LISTEN TO ME!

DON'T EVER DOUBT.
WHA......
EVEN IF THERE ARE TIMES WHEN WE DON'T KNOW WHERE THE OTHER IS...
DON'T LOSE SIGHT OF YOURSELF.
DON'T HESITATE.
DON'T LET YOUR THOUGHTS RUN LIKE THAT.
DON'T WAVER.
SHINING SO INTENSELY...
—IF YOU CAN DO THAT... THEN...
GU
...ALWAYS LIKE THE SUN.

...I WILL
COME BACK
TO YOU.

I WILL NOT LET GO OF THIS LIFE THAT EASILY...
...SHUUSEI—
...IF I HAVE A PARTNER WHO TRUSTS ME AND WAITS FOR ME.
GOT IT?
THEN BE GOOD AND WAIT FOR ME.

AND DON'T THINK ABOUT TRYING TO COME ALONG, EITHER.
WHA!?
NO WAY! I WASN'T GONNA TRY THAT!
I WAS ONLY THINKIN' ABOUT IT FOR HALF A SECOND!
YOU DID THINK ABOUT IT, THOUGH...
QUIT IT, THIS IS EMBAR-RASSING.
BECAUSE SHUUSEI SAYS HE'LL COME BACK.
WAIT UP...
...SHUU-SEI!
THIS JUMPY NERVOUS FEELING IN MY CHEST...
—HE'LL BE OKAY...
IT'S JUST MY IMAGINATION.
PICHA (PLISH)

GATA
ガタ
GATA
ガタ
GATA
ガタ
GATA (SHAKE)
ガタ
H......
HELP ME...
P... PLEASE DON'T KILL ME!
PLEASE! I'M SORRY!
I-I'LL DO ANYTHING...!
CHAPU (SPLISH)

ZABU (SPLASH)
TO DIE!
ZABAN (KA-SPLASH)
AAAH! I'M SORRY! I DON'T WANT TO DIE! I DON'T WANT TO DIE! I DON'T
ZU (PLUNGE)
GOBO (BURBLE)
GOBO
GOBO
Story 43 • END

THE
BETRAYAL
KNOWS MY NAME

THE DISTANT PAST OF THE ZWEILT

ON THE NIGHT OF STORY 20

IT BEGAN WITH A LITTLE QUESTION I HAD.

HAVE ALL OF THE ZWEILT...

...ALWAYS BEEN PAIRED WITH THE SAME PARTNERS, FOR ALL THEIR PAST LIVES?

UM—

WELL, WE HAVE...

AND ALL THE MEMBERS HERE HAVE.

BUT THERE ARE ALSO ZWEILT WHO LOST THEIR PARTNERS IN BATTLE...

...AND WENT ON TO FIGHT ALONE, OR TO FIND A NEW PARTNER.

WENT ON TO FIGHT ALONE ...?

SO YOU CAN'T JUST TRAIN AN-OTHER...

...TO BECOME A ZWEILT?

OF COURSE YOU CAN!☆ IF SOMEONE HAS THE INBORN TALENT FOR IT.
OTHERWISE, NO MATTER HOW MUCH TRAINING THEY GET, IT'S NO USE.
PERSONNEL REPLACEMENT ISN'T THAT SIMPLE, YOU SEE.
AND IT'S NOT OFTEN THAT PEOPLE WITH THE TALENT FOR IT COME ALONG.
ZWEILT REALLY ARE AMAZING.
OH, YEAH...
...ISN'T THAT WHY WE TRIED TO HAVE BABIES ONCE?
BAKO!! (KLONK!!)
OWWW! WHAT WAS THAT FOR!?
YOU HIT ME WITH A BOOK!!
THAT WAS IN A PAST LIFE!! WILL YOU THINK ABOUT HOW THINGS SOUND BEFORE YOU TALK!?
THAT WAS JUST A LITTLE AWKWARD!!
...
...
THAT WAS A VERY LONG TIME AGO.
HEE HEE.
...THE ZWEILT WERE DWINDLING IN NUMBERS...
...AND WE HAD TO TRY AND REPRODUCE ON PURPOSE—
OOOH. I GET IT!
ONE OF YOU USED TO BE A LADY!
YEP.
IT WAS SHUUSEI.
WHAAAAAAAT!?
FOR REAL!?

OH, I SEE.
SO YOU THOUGHT THAT A CHILD BORN TO TWO ZWEILT WOULD SURELY INHERIT THAT TALENT.
WAS THAT HOW IT WENT?
YEAH, WELL...
THE HIGHER-UPS THOUGHT OF IT...
BUT IN THE END YOU DIDN'T HAVE ANY CHILDREN...
NOT ONE...
NOPE...
TO MAKE ZWEILT—...
SO...
HOW WAS SHE? THE LADY VERSION OF SHUU-KUN MUST HAVE BEEN QUITE A BABE, HUH?
← BRAGGING.
YOU KNOW IT! A HOTTIE TO SURPASS ALL HOTTIES!
I WON'T NEVER FORGET.
OOOH, WISH I COULD'VE MET HER!
FORGET IT.
IT MIGHT'VE BEEN ME BUT IT'S NOT NOW.
OH—
I BET IF YOU DRESSED UP LIKE A LADY NOW YOU'D STILL BE PRETTY.
WANNA TRY IT?
YOU'RE NOT HAPPY WITH ME THE WAY I AM!?

SO, THEN...
YOU TWO ARE MARRIED?
NO!!
THAT WAS A PAST LIFE! IN THE PAST!!
ARE YOU SURE?
?
VERY SURE!!
HA HA HA HA
THEN WHY DO YOU HANG ALL OVER ONE AN-OTHER?
WHO'S DOING THAT!?
YEAH, YOU'RE ONE TO TALK!
AH HA HA HA HA
WHERE DOES ONE...
...EVEN START...
...SURE, WHAT-EVER...
HEY! HOLD UP!
YOU WANNA GO!?
STOP THAT, YOU TWO! NO POINTLESS FIGHTING!
MUST BE NICE...
HUH?
THE FIGHT-ING?
I'VE NEVER BEEN MARRIED TO TOOKO-CHAN...
IT'S NIGHT-TIME, TOOMA-SAN...
OH, LOOK, THE WEATHER IS SO CLEAR AND LOVELY, YUKI-SAN!!
THE MORE I DISCOVER ABOUT THE ZWEILT, THE MORE COMPLICATED THEY ARE.
SO I DECIDED NOT TO ASK ANY MORE QUESTIONS...
AH AH HA HA HA HA HA HA HA HA

Night of Story 20 • END

AFTERWORD - BEHIND THE SCENES OF URABOKU.

IT'S BEEN A WHILE! I'M GLAD TO SEE YOU ALL AGAIN.

SO URABOKU 9 IS FINALLY OUT.

THIS AFTERWORD... I FEAR IT'LL ONLY ADD TO MY SHAME.

I THOUGHT OF NOT DOING ONE... BUT MY EDITOR SAID TO WRITE IT ANYWAY...

I TOOK A BREAK FROM THE SERIAL PUBLICATION FOR A WHILE.

THERE WERE A LOT OF PROBLEMS FOR ME LAST YEAR...

...BUT THE WORST WAS THAT OLD ACQUAINTANCE OF MINE, TENDONITIS.

PORO (DROP)

I THOUGHT I COULD JUST WORK THROUGH THE PAIN BUT THEN I COULDN'T EVEN HOLD A PEN.

I DON'T WANT TO WRITE ABOUT SUCH DEPRESSING THINGS, BUT...

IS THIS GOING TO BE...

...THE END OF MY CAREER?

THAT'S REALLY WHAT I WAS THINKING.

SFX: ZUKI (THROB) ZUKI

TO EVERYONE WHO SAID THEY WERE SAD AND BEGGED ME TO RESUME SOON—THANK YOU!

BECAUSE OF YOU ALL, I DIDN'T LOSE HOPE.

SO WHEN I GOT BACK TO WORK ON IT, I THOUGHT, FIRST OF ALL I'LL RESPOND TO SOME READERS' REQUESTS.

AND THAT'S WHY YUKI AND THE OTHERS WENT TO A HOT SPRING.

I'VE GOTTEN A LOT OF "I WANT EVERYONE TO GO ON A TRIP TOGETHER" AND "PLEASE GIVE LUKA A BATH SCENE!"... SO, THERE'S ONE WAY TO KILL THOSE TWO BIRDS WITH ONE STONE. IT'S GOTTA BE... A HOT SPRING.

WELL THEY'RE CERTAINLY DIRECT......

IT HASN'T REALLY GOTTEN BETTER, BECAUSE IT'S CHRONIC BY NOW!

BUT PLEASE DON'T WORRY!

I WANT TO DRAW MANGA NO MATTER HOW PAINFUL IT GETS, SO, THERE'S NOTHING FOR IT.

THAT'S WHY ALL OF VOLUME 9 IS KIND OF LIKE A SIDE STORY.

AND IN ASUKA THE MAIN STORY IS MAKING PROGRESS.

SO PLEASE TAKE A LOOK IF YOU'RE INTERESTED!

AND I HAD A SIGNING.

THANK YOU TO EVERYONE WHO CAME! ♡

THERE WERE EVEN PEOPLE WHO CAME ALL THE WAY FROM FINLAND...

OH, AND THERE WERE GUYS TOO!

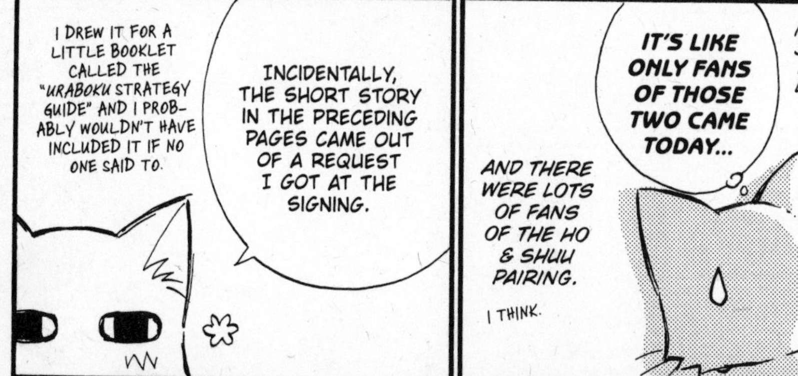

I GUESS THIS IS WHY THEY'RE GETTING MORE PAGE TIME...

I TOTALLY FORGOT ABOUT IT...

ANYWAY, I THINK SOME OF YOU MUST ALREADY KNOW THIS, BUT URABOKU IS GETTING A THEATER PRODUCTION.
WHA— A PLAY? LIKE ON STAGE? HOW!?
I MEAN, ISN'T THAT WHAT YOU'D WANT TO KNOW?
YUKI AND LUKA...
...APPEARING BEFORE MY EYES AS REAL-LIFE PEOPLE— I NEVER EVEN DREAMED OF IT!
THE ACTORS MUST BE REALLY COOL...
I'M TOTALLY SHOCKED— AND I TOTALLY CAN'T WAIT TO SEE IT!
AND THEY'RE DOING IT FOR CHRISTMAS— KIND OF ROMANTIC, RIGHT?
PLEASE THINK OF IT AS A SPECIAL OCCASION AND GO SEE THE SHOW, EVERYONE!
IT'S A ONCE-IN-A-LIFETIME KINDA THING!
IT'S GONNA BE WONDERFUL!
I'LL BE DOING AN ILLUSTRATION FOR THE TICKETS!
SINCE IT IS A SPECIAL OCCASION...

ABOUT VOLUME 10!
I MIGHT BE GETTING AHEAD OF MYSELF HERE, BUT VOLUME 10 IS COMING OUT NEXT.
IT IS TOO EARLY. UU
AND THERE'LL BE A SPECIAL MEMORIAL LIMITED EDITION!
IT'LL COME WITH A DRAMA CD OF A LITTLE SIDE SCENARIO.
I'M WRITING THE SCRIPT... SPECIALLY FOR THIS...
AND, AND! THE THINGS THAT DIDN'T MAKE IT INTO THE MANGA BEFORE... AND STUFF I HAD TO PUT OFF BECAUSE OF PAGE CONSTRAINTS... THEY LET ME PUT IT IN HERE...
WHICH IS TO SAY, THE CONTENTS ARE TOTALLY TIED IN WITH THE MAIN STORY...SO, WHAT I'M SAYING IS— I'M SAYING—
PLEASE, IF YOU CAN, PLEEEEAASE LISTEN TO IT!!
※A SCREAM FROM DEEP WITHIN MY SOUL.
THE STORY HAS TO DO WITH SECRETS FROM YUKI'S PAST LIFE, SO IF WE CAN GET THE VOICE ACTORS TO DO IT, IT SHOULD BE AMAZING.
ALTHOUGH I MUST BE SOME KIND OF IDIOT FOR LEAVING STUFF LIKE THAT OUT OF THE MANGA...
BUT IT SOUNDS REALLY GREAT AS AN AUDIO DRAMA... AT LEAST THAT'S WHAT I'D LIKE PEOPLE TO SAY.
IT'LL COME WITH A SPECIAL PRESENT TOO! ♡ IT'S A SERIOUSLY CUTE AND GORGEOUS TOTE BAG. THE BLACK BUNNY WAS A TOTAL STICKLER FOR IT.
I WANNA INCLUDE SOME MERCH WITH IT THAT NOBODY ELSE EVER INCLUDES! SOMETHING SPECIAL!
SAID THIS THE WHOLE TIME.
I SAW THE PROTOTYPE! IT HAS LAMÉ, AND IT'S ALL SPARKLY! IT'S SO PRETTY! AND A LOVELY PURPLE PRINT—I REALLY LIKE IT!
AND APART FROM THE COVER, I'M WRITING AN AFTERWORD TOO.
BEHIND THE SCENES OF URABOKU.
SO IF YOU HAVE ANY QUESTIONS FOR ME, NOW'S YOUR CHANCE—PLEASE WRITE ME A LETTER!
AND I'LL ANSWER THEM IN THE AFTERWORD IF I CAN...

AND IN THIS ONE, FOR THE FIRST TIME IN A WHILE, THERE'S AN OFFSHOT CARD (THE FIFTH ONE) WITH THE FIRST PRINTING OF SENSHIROU-SAN.
AS FOR THE SITUATION— A DECISION WAS REACHED BETWEEN REQUESTS AND DISCUSSIONS WITH MY EDITOR...
FOR MY PART, I WANTED TO DRAW KUROTO DOZING OFF...
AMBUSHING HIM IN BED... FROM AN OUTSIDE PERSPECTIVE IT KINDA ALMOST LOOKS CREEPY ....
WELL, I DREW IT, BUT...
WELL, I WOULDN'T MIND MUCH IF SENSHIROU-SAN DID THAT TO ME—
I LIIIIKE HIM! ♥

AND THEN, AT THE END OF THE VOLUME, WE PUT IN SOME CHARACTER PROFILES AND A LITTLE WORLDBUILDING BACKGROUND.
IT FEELS LIKE IT MUST BE ANNOYING TO GO ON AND ON ABOUT MY OWN CHARACTERS...
...SO I HAVEN'T DONE THAT BEFORE...
BUT I'M STILL NOT SURE HOW MUCH OF THEM REALLY COMES THROUGH IN THE STORY...
...SO I TRIED WRITING UP SOME LITTLE BLURBS ABOUT THEM.
WHEN THERE'S SOME EXTRA PAGE SPACE I'LL GET TO THE OTHER CHARACTERS TOO.

THANK YOU FOR READING, EVERYONE!
HOPE I SEE YOU NEXT TIME!

BEHIND THE SCENES OF

SPECIAL THANKS

✝

K-san

H.Sanbe

H.Matsuo

T.Kondo

R.Mozai

C.Sudo

K.Okuda

E.Yamagishi

K.Kato

Y.Suzuki

...... and You

SEND LETTERS TO:

✤ HOTARU ODAGIRI
C/O GEKKAN ASUKA EDITORIAL DEPARTMENT
KADOKAWA SHOTEN, INC.
TOKYO, JAPAN 102-8078

RECENTLY THERE WAS KIND OF A CLUSTER OF LETTERS FROM OLDER FANS...A GENERATION REMOVED FROM THE READERS WHO USUALLY SEND ME LETTERS! AND SO MANY ALL OF A SUDDEN! ✧

I DON'T KNOW WHY THEY ALL CAME AT ONCE LIKE THAT, BUT IT WAS A HAPPY SURPRISE~ ✿

THEY WROTE THAT IT GAVE THEM COURAGE! ✿

I'M SO GRATE-FUL...

DATA
Birthday ▶ April 21
(Actually, when he was taken in by Morning Sun House)
Zodiac sign ▶ Taurus
Age ▶ 16
Blood type ▶ O
Height ▶ 169 cm
Hobbies ▶ Martial arts, go, and shogi (all taught to him by the headmaster at Morning Sun House)
Favorite food ▶ White rice, fish
Least favorite food ▶ Sour, vinegary things
Special ability ▶ Light of God
Yuki Giou

Since I wanted to tell a love story, Yuki was at first going to be a girl. But the editors said, make the main character a boy, we don't want a love story. So I moaned and wept and made it a boy, and that's the Yuki you see here. Still, I couldn't get myself to abandon the element of romance, so I went with my instinct and made him a girl in his past life... But once I began the series, I realized it would be pretty tough to execute. I think I was too naive. Now I feel like that complexity, falling into the labyrinth of overthinking things, is what makes *Uraboku*. Yuki is a walking mass of inferiority complexes. And since he was abandoned, left to an orphanage, he has this really fierce desire to feel needed, to be loved. But we all have that desire, more or less, don't we? I wanted to write a character who shows that.

DATA
Birthday ▶ –
Zodiac sign ▶ –
Age ▶ Appears 18 to 20
Blood type ▶ –
Height ▶ 189 cm
Hobbies ▶ None
Favorite foods ▶ Junk food
Least favorite food ▶ Nothing, really
Name of weapon ▶ ROXASS
Luka Crosszeria

I've never drawn this type of character before—the sexy type, to be frank, flawlessly handsome. And I think I created him on a reckless whim—hey, why not give it a shot? Really, really reckless of me... And I angsted over that from the start too, with the awareness that people have different tastes and priorities! (Though in my defense, I really didn't have a lot of time to get everything ready before the serialization started...) Since he was kind of too perfect, I gave him a weird palate and made him love terrible junk food. As for what Luka is really like, that's something I'll have to go into more and more from here on out. He's a person who persists in loving another even through the hardest times, but that's not just him—there are other characters in *Uraboku* who do that, or at least try to. So look for them too. And incidentally, most of the Luka fans say that they can forgive his love interest since he's a boy now... (LOL)

DATA

Birthday ▶ June 22
Zodiac sign ▶ Cancer
Age ▶ 17
Blood type ▶ A
Height ▶ 165 cm
Hobbies ▶ Accessorizing, making sweets
Favorite food ▶ Pasta
Least favorite food ▶ Organs, spicy things
Name of weapon ▶ Eon
Special ability ▶ Ear of God
Alias ▶ The One Who Inquires

Tooko Murasame

I had a feeling that the two main characters would turn out to be tough to draw, so I created these siblings with the idea that they should be easier to handle. And I was right. In both looks and personality Tooko is terribly easy to work with (although her long straight hair does take a lot of effort to ink). I draw her with the sense that she's the most "normal" of the cast. She likes sweets, she's stylish, she worries about her weight and goes on diets, but she gets frustrated too, and she's interested in romance... She's a pretty typical high school girl, the sort you'd find in every class. But this same girl is burdened with the fate of having to fight in a war. That normal everyday life is dear to her because she might lose it at any time, and she lives in it with her whole being. Readers often tell me they envy her, having a brother like Tsukumo.

DATA
Birthday ▶ October 10
Zodiac sign ▶ Libra
Age ▶ 15
Blood type ▶ O
Height ▶ 177 cm
Hobbies ▶ Tennis, caring for animals
Favorite foods ▶ Sweet things, fruit
Least favorite food ▶ Things that smell strongly
Name of weapon ▶ Knell
Special ability ▶ Ear of God
Alias ▶ The One Who Inquires
Tsukumo Murasame

Aside from the main characters, Tsukumo was the first character whose design and personality I finished. Readers often say it must be hard to draw Tsukumo's hair, and it isn't all that easy... He's easy to write in his personality and moods, though. Since he can hear a little too much, he hears what people don't say, and he's been hurt deeply by people speaking thoughtlessly. (Tooko's Ear of God ability isn't as strong as his. She can't hear people's thoughts or talk to animals.) He's a guy who's nice to people when he's been hurt. He doesn't say much, but he isn't shy or hesitant about showing kindness. He's generous with his love, particularly to his sister Tooko. He's the type of character to have a high approval rating with teenage girls.

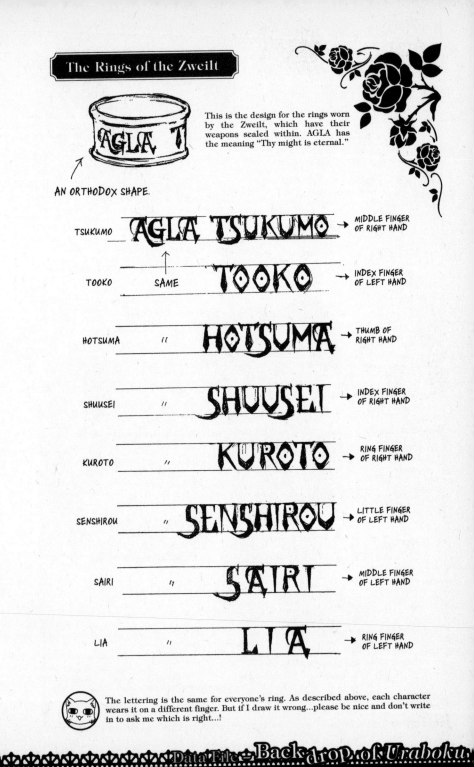

The Rings of the Zweilt

This is the design for the rings worn by the Zweilt, which have their weapons sealed within. AGLA has the meaning "Thy might is eternal."

AN ORTHODOX SHAPE.

TSUKUMO	AGLA	TSUKUMO	→ MIDDLE FINGER OF RIGHT HAND
TOOKO	SAME	TOOKO	→ INDEX FINGER OF LEFT HAND
HOTSUMA	"	HOTSUMA	→ THUMB OF RIGHT HAND
SHUUSEI	"	SHUUSEI	→ INDEX FINGER OF RIGHT HAND
KUROTO	"	KUROTO	→ RING FINGER OF RIGHT HAND
SENSHIROU	"	SENSHIROU	→ LITTLE FINGER OF LEFT HAND
SAIRI	"	SAIRI	→ MIDDLE FINGER OF LEFT HAND
LIA	"	LIA	→ RING FINGER OF LEFT HAND

The lettering is the same for everyone's ring. As described above, each character wears it on a different finger. But if I draw it wrong...please be nice and don't write in to ask me which is right...!

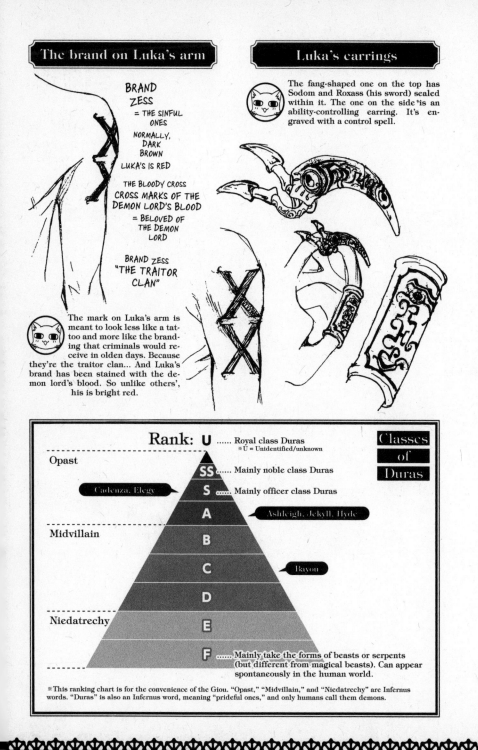

The brand on Luka's arm

BRAND ZESS
= THE SINFUL ONES
NORMALLY, DARK BROWN
LUKA'S IS RED
THE BLOODY CROSS
CROSS MARKS OF THE DEMON LORD'S BLOOD
= BELOVED OF THE DEMON LORD
BRAND ZESS
"THE TRAITOR CLAN"

The mark on Luka's arm is meant to look less like a tattoo and more like the branding that criminals would receive in olden days. Because they're the traitor clan... And Luka's brand has been stained with the demon lord's blood. So unlike others', his is bright red.

Luka's earrings

The fang-shaped one on the top has Sodom and Roxass (his sword) sealed within it. The one on the side is an ability-controlling earring. It's engraved with a control spell.

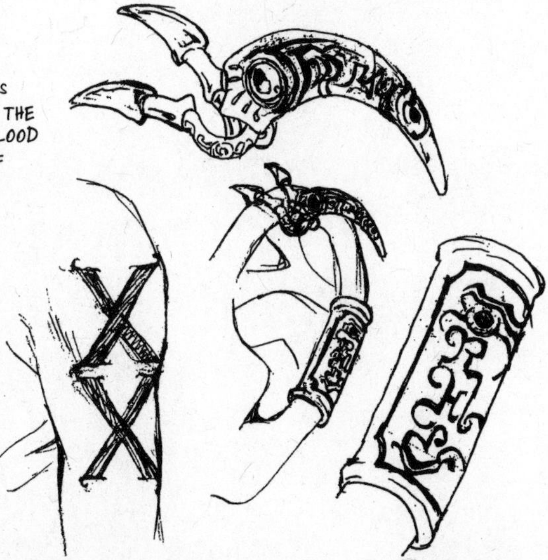

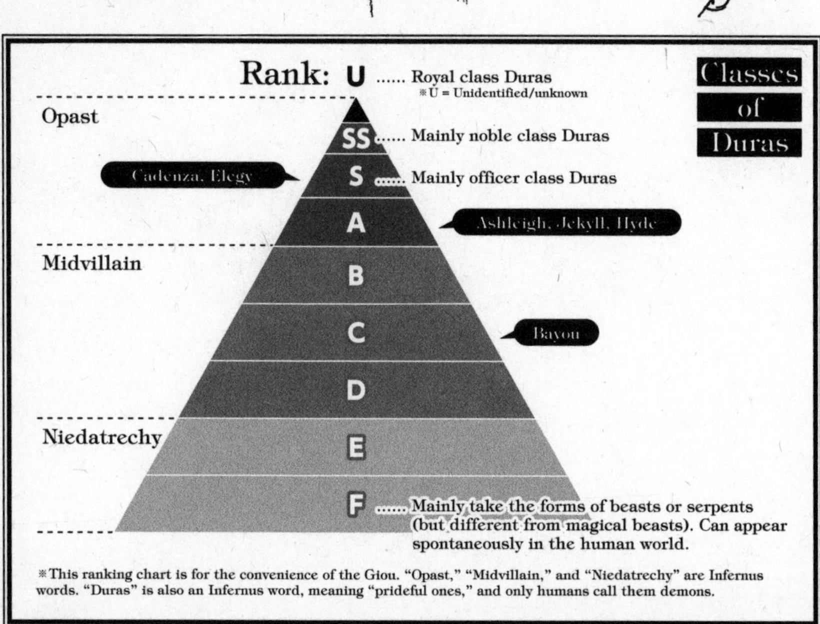

※This ranking chart is for the convenience of the Giou. "Opast," "Midvillain," and "Niedatrechy" are Infernus words. "Duras" is also an Infernus word, meaning "prideful ones," and only humans call them demons.

The
BETRAYAL
knows my name

Early this morning, a young man's body...
...was found floating in Shinobazu Pond in Ueno Park in Taitou City.
The body has been identified as that of Naohiro Koyama, a third-year student at the Taito City public middle school.
He appears to have drowned.
Naohiro Koyama (15)
The police are investigating whether it was an accident or—
KUH KUH KUH ...!
JUST LOOK AT YOU NOW, KOYAMA ...!
I'LL KILL THEM...
I'LL KILL EVERY LAST ONE OF THEM...!
BUT THEY WON'T CATCH ME...

Story 44
TOKYO,
THE
DEMON
CAPITAL

THE
BETRAYAL
KNOWS MY NAME

Early this morning, a young man's body...
...was found floating in Shinobazu Pond in Ueno Park in Taitou City.
The body has been identified as that of Naohiro Koyama, a third-year student at the Taito City public middle school.
He appears to have drowned.
Naohiro Koyama (15)
The police are investigating whether it was an accident or—
KUH KUH KUH ...!
JUST LOOK AT YOU NOW, KOYAMA ...!
I'LL KILL THEM...
I'LL KILL EVERY LAST ONE OF THEM...!
BUT THEY WON'T CATCH ME...

Story 44
TOKYO,
THE
DEMON
CAPITAL

THE
BETRAYAL
KNOWS MY NAME

SHINOBAZU POND, UENO
SHINOBAZU POND IS ONLY ABOUT NINETY CENTIMETERS DEEP.
IT'S DIFFICULT TO IMAGINE ANYONE NOT A SMALL CHILD ACCIDENTALLY DROWNING IN IT.
THAT'S TRUE...
AS FAR BACK AS I CAN REMEMBER, ONLY ONE OR TWO PEOPLE HAVE DIED IN THIS POND—
—THE BOY WHO DIED, KOYAMA—
HE WASN'T DRUNK OR TAKING SLEEPING PILLS OR ANYTHING, WAS HE?
NO, SIR. NOTHING LIKE THAT TURNED UP IN THE AU-TOPSY.

KEEP OUT
KEEP OUT
WE WOULD SUSPECT MURDER OR SUICIDE...
...BUT THERE ARE NO INJURIES, NO SIGNS OF A STRUGGLE.
AND HE DIDN'T LEAVE A NOTE... WELL, THIS WOULD BE A WEIRD PLACE FOR A SUICIDE, ANYWAY.
NORMALLY, WE'D WRITE THIS ONE OFF AS AN ACCIDENT.
I SEE...
THEN, ABOUT THE OTHER INCIDENT...
OH— YES, SIR.
TEN DAYS AGO, OVER THE EDGE OF THE TEMPLE UP AHEAD THERE, THE KIYOMIZU-KANNON-DOU...
...A BODY TURNED UP.
ALSO A THIRD YEAR AT ENJU MIDDLE SCHOOL— TAKUYA MASUDA.
AND HE WAS IN THE SAME LITTLE DELINQUENT GANG THAT KOYAMA RAN WITH.
SO THE REASON WE CONTACTED YOU IS THAT THESE DEATHS OCCURRED ONE AFTER THE OTHER—
AND, WELL, I DON'T KNOW MUCH ABOUT IT, BUT...
THERE'LL BE SOME KIND OF TROUBLE IF TOO MANY PEOPLE END UP DYING IN THE PARK?

...YES. IT WOULD BE TROUBLE.
FOR ALL JAPAN...
WHA...?
THOUGH THE TAKUYA MASUDA CASE WAS WRITTEN OFF AS A SUICIDE...
OH— YEAH, IT WAS.
THOUGH AT FIRST THEY FIGURED IT FOR AN ACCIDENT...
YOU CAN PROBABLY TELL, BUT THIS TEMPLE WAS BUILT ON THE PATTERN OF THE FAMOUS KIYOMIZUDERA IN KYOTO.
SO WE THOUGHT MAYBE HE WAS TAKING A FLYING LEAP OFF THE KIYOMIZUDERA STAGE, AS THE SAYING GOES.
INCI-DENTAL-LY...
...EVEN IF HE HAD TRIPPED, BENEATH THE RAILING...
...THERE'S A WALKWAY CLOSED OFF WITH AN IRON FENCE.
HE COULDN'T HAVE FALLEN ALL THE WAY DOWN THE BLUFF.

FOR SOMEBODY TO FALL OFF THE BLUFF...
...THEY COULDN'T JUST *TRIP*.
THEY'D HAVE TO MAKE A CONSCIOUS EFFORT TO JUMP REALLY FAR.
—THEN YOU'RE SAYING IT HAD TO HAVE BEEN SUICIDE.
RIGHT... BUT IT STILL DOESN'T ADD UP.
SURE, THERE'S A BLUFF, BUT IT'S NOT ALL THAT HIGH, AND THERE ARE GRASS AND TREES ALL OVER IT.
AND YET IT LOOKED LIKE MASUDA DIED ON IMPACT. HIS BODY WAS WRECKED PRETTY BADLY.
LESS LIKE HE FELL FROM THE RAILING...
...AND MORE LIKE HE SOMEHOW HIT THE GROUND AT TREMENDOUS SPEED—...
...I SEE.
SO EVEN IF IT IS SUICIDE, QUITE A FEW QUESTIONS STILL REMAIN... AND NOW, THERE'S BEEN ANOTHER INCIDENT, WITH NAOHIRO KOYAMA.
BUT AT THIS POINT WE DON'T KNOW WHETHER THEY ARE CONNECTED—IS THAT RIGHT?
THAT'S RIGHT...
ACCIDENT, MURDER, SUICIDE...
FRANKLY, IF THERE ARE ANY DEITIES AROUND HERE, I WISH THEY'D POINT ME IN THE RIGHT DIRECTION.

—FIND ANYTHING, TSUKUMO?
...NO. NOTHING, SIR.
HFF...
THERE ARE NO HUMAN VOICES AROUND HERE THAT SOUND LIKE KOYAMA-KUN.
ARE YOU ALL RIGHT, TSUKUMO-KUN?
OVERDID IT WITH THE "EAR OF GOD" THERE?
FURA (WOBBLE)
YEAH... A LITTLE... LOOKS LIKE I'VE BEEN PICKING UP TOO MUCH NOISE...
BUT I'M FINE.
WITH SHUUSEI GONE, I'LL HAVE TO DO ALL I CAN...
TAKASHIRO-SAMA, COULD I TRY THE BELONGINGS OF THE DECEASED NEXT, SIR?
VERY WELL.
WE'D LIKE TO TAKE A LOOK AT NAOHIRO KOYAMA'S BELONGINGS.
ABSO-LUTELY.
BACK TO THE STATION, THEN—
BRING THE CAR OVER.
......

HEY, TSUKUMO, DON'T PUSH YOURSELF TOO HARD.
YAMATO... OH, YEAH, MASAMUNE'S LITTLE BROTHER...
HE PASSED AWAY JUST THIS SPRING, DIDN'T HE.
UH-HUH.
...HEY, ISN'T ENJU MIDDLE WHERE YAMATO-KUN WENT TO SCHOOL?
YEAH...
THREE STUDENTS IN A ROW, FROM THE SAME SCHOOL...
CAN THAT BE A COINCIDENCE?
DUNNO...
GUESS THAT'S WHAT WE'RE SUPPOSED TO FIND OUT.
WHEN WE LISTEN TO HIS BELONGINGS, IT SHOULD START TO BECOME CLEAR WHETHER THERE'S SOMETHING MORE TO IT.
TRUE...
—IT'D BE NICE IF IT DIDN'T INVOLVE A DURAS, THOUGH.
BUBUBU (VVVT)

A TEXT MESSAGE... FROM TOOKO-CHAN.
SHE'S SIGHT-SEEING IN KYOTO NOW.
YOU TWO TEXT EACH OTHER ABOUT EVERY TINY LITTLE THING!!
UGH!
YOU MIGHT SAY THAT, BUT... SHE WROTE ABOUT SHUUSEI TOO.
YOU DON'T WANT TO KNOW WHAT IT SAYS? YOU DO, DON'T YOU?
SEE? SEE?
COME ON, YOU TWO!
I— I DON'T CARE!!
SO THIS WEEK HOTSUMA-KUN AND TSUKUMO-KUN WILL WORK AS A PAIR?
—OH, I SEE.
YUP ♪
JUST UNTIL SHUU-KUN AND TOOKO-CHAN GET BACK FROM THEIR TRIP.
SHUUSEI-KUN AND TOOKO-CHAN ARE ON A WEEKLONG CLASS TRIP.

AND RII-KUN WENT TO GET YOU FROM SCHOOL, RIGHT?

SINCE HE CAME HOME SAYING THE SHOOT ENDED EARLY.

YES...

...AND SENSHIROU-SAN CAME IN THE CAR TOO—

THEN I SAID GOODBYE TO HOTSUMA-KUN, TSUKUMO-KUN, AND LIA-CHAN...

...AND I CAME HOME WITH KUROTO-KUN AND SENSHIROU-SAN.

BECAUSE THE GENERAL RULE IS ZWEILT ACT IN PAIRS, OF COURSE!

BUT...

...WHY IS UENO PARK SUCH AN IMPORTANT PLACE?

EVEN TAKASHIRO-SAN WENT, DIDN'T HE ...?

AHH...

WELL, THERE'S A *BARRIER* THERE, WHICH THE GIOU FAMILY DEFENDS.

A BARRIER ...?

YES. AND NOT JUST IN UENO.

THE GIOU HAVE PUT UP BARRIERS AT ALL THE INAUSPICIOUS SPOTS—THE SO-CALLED "EVIL SPIRIT GATES" OF TOKYO.

LONG AGO—THAT IS, BACK WHEN TOKYO WAS STILL CALLED EDO...
OF COURSE, THE "EVIL SPIRITS" WERE ACTUALLY DURAS.
...THE GIOU WERE REQUESTED BY THE SHOGUNATE TO PREVENT EVIL SPIRITS FROM COMING AND GOING...
...AND SO THEY WENT AROUND THE CITY SETTING UP BARRIERS OF SPIRITUAL POWER.
YOU CAN THINK OF DURAS AS CREATURES THAT LIVE IN A DIFFERENT DIMENSION FROM THIS ONE.
AND THERE ARE PLACES WHERE IT IS EASY TO CONNECT THE DIMENSION WHERE HUMANS LIVE TO THE DIMENSION WHERE DURAS LIVE.
AND THOSE SPOTS CAME TO BE CALLED THE "EVIL SPIRIT GATES."
TO SEAL OFF THE EVIL SPIRIT GATES, A BARRIER HAS TO BE PUT UP, AND THE LAND THERE MUST ALWAYS BE KEPT IN A STATE OF PURITY.

—KEPT IN A STATE OF PURITY...
RIGHT! SO, IN SUCH CASES, SHRINES OR TEMPLES ARE OFTEN ERECTED, YOU KNOW.
UENO PARK HAD A TEMPLE THERE TO START WITH.
THEN, FOR SOMEONE TO DIE IN ONE OF THOSE SPOTS...
IT'S REALLY NOT GOOD! IF MORE PEOPLE DIE THERE, IT TAINTS THE LAND AND THE BARRIER HAS TO BE RECON-STRUCTED.
—WELL, ACCIDENTAL DEATH ISN'T SO BAD, BUT...
THE REAL PROBLEM IS MURDER.
UNLIKE AN ACCIDENTAL DEATH...
...THINGS LIKE MALICE AND NEGATIVE EMOTIONS LINGER THERE.
A LOVELY FEAST FOR THE DURAS.
IN THE BLINK OF AN EYE, THE LAND IS TAINTED AND THE BARRIER BROKEN...
...AND A "HOLE" OPENS UP, CONNECTING TO IN-FERNUS—

TOKYO, WHERE SO MANY PEOPLE ARE CONCENTRATED, IT'S A NEVER-ENDING WHIRL OF POLITICAL SCHEMING AND ALL THE COMPLICATIONS OF HUMAN RELATIONSHIPS.
IT'S KNOWN AS A PLACE WHERE ILL WILL AND NEGATIVITY TEND TO ACCUMULATE—ONE OF THE MOST SPIRITUALLY DANGEROUS PLACES IN THE WORLD.
THAT'S WHY THE GIOU STRIVE TO TAKE VERY GOOD CARE OF THE BARRIERS.
THEN...
...IF THE BARRIER IS BROKEN, THAT WOULD MEAN BIG TROUBLE FOR TOKYO...
NAAAH, IT'LL BE FINE!
THERE ARE BARRIERS ALL OVER THE PLACE, REALLY~! ♪
EVEN IF ONE OR TWO FALL, ONLY NIEDATRECHY WOULD COME OUT, OR MIDVILLAIN AT THE WORST...
EITHER WAY, THE ZWEILT AND LUKA-KUN WOULD TAKE CARE OF THEM, NO PROBLEM! ♥
WELL, I GUESS IT WOULD KIIINDA BE A PROBLEM...

—BESIDES...
...WITH THE MOST POWERFUL PEOPLE IN THE GIOU CLAN HERE...
THAT IS, TAKASHIRO-SAN, AND YOU, YUKI-KUN—THE BARRIERS ALL OVER JAPAN WILL HOLD STRONG.
M...
ME?
THAT'S RIGHT!☆ I HEAR THE LIGHT OF GOD IS A "BARRIER DEFENSE" SPECIALIST, YOU KNOW!
BUT I'M JUST...AN ORDINARY HUMAN......
AH HA HA HA HA HA!
SERIOUSLY!? YOU'RE SUCH A JOKER!
THE LIGHT OF GOD, ORDINARY!!
BAN (BANG)
ぼんぼんっ
BAN
989...
990...
POTA (DRIP)
ポタ
991...

993...
992...
コツ
KOTSU (TOK)
ガチャーン
GACHAN (CLANK)
KUROTO.
AREN'T YOU OVERDOING IT A LITTLE?
YOU'VE BEEN WORKING OUT EVER SINCE WE GOT HOME...

......SEN-SHIROU.
DID YOU FINISH YOUR ILLUSTRATION PROJECT?
DON'T YOU HAVE A DEAD-LINE?
I DID, THANKS.
...IS IT FOR THAT NOVEL SERIES AGAIN?
THE ONE WITH THE SHRINE MAIDEN AND THE GUY IN GLASSES AND THE GIRL WITH CAT EARS AND ALL THAT...
OH, YOU REMEMBERED!
DOSU (TUNK)
WHAT GENRE IS THAT EVEN SUPPOSED TO BE?
HMM... I'M NOT REALLY SURE MY-SELF.
I JUST LOOKED AT THE REFERENCES AND DREW WHAT I WAS TOLD, AND IT'S POPULAR NOW...
...DON'T YOU SPECIALIZE IN JAPANESE PAINTING?
YES, BUT IT'S ALSO FUN TO DRAW THINGS THAT I WOULDN'T NORMALLY DRAW.
HMMM...
WHAT ABOUT YOU? YOU DIDN'T HAVE ANY CLUB ACTIVI-TIES TODAY, RIGHT?
HOW IS IT? THE GO AND SHOGI CLUB—
ARE YOU HAVING FUN?

PASA (FWUP)
...I'M REGRETTING IT.
I SHOULDN'T HAVE JOINED.
I...NEVER SHOULD HAVE STARTED GOING TO HIGH SCHOOL IN THE FIRST PLACE.
....
...WHY NOT?

—......
YAAAY! WE MADE IT THROUGH THE SECOND ROUND!!
ALL THANKS TO YOU, HOURAI-KUN!!
ALL THAT...
WE WANNA PLAY SHOGI WITH YOUUU!
...LAUGHING WITHOUT A CARE...
...AND PASSING THE TIME TOGETHER...
LIKE... A NORMAL PERSON WITH FRIENDS...
BUT ISN'T IT NICE TO HAVE FRIENDS?
I DON'T WANT ANY.
IT JUST MAKES ME SOFT.

......
...YOU'VE BEEN IN HERE LATELY, TRAINING SO HARD IT LOOKS LIKE YOU'RE HURTING YOURSELF ...?
IS THAT WHY...
KUROTO......
......WHY...
...WOULD I BE GIVEN TIME LIKE THIS......?
MY HEART IS STILL...FILLED UP WITH POISON.
ANGER AND HATE.
I HAVEN'T FORGOTTEN.
THERE'S NO WAY I CAN FORGET.
—BUT...
...THIS TRAN-QUIL-LITY...
...THIS WARMTH—IT PARALYZES SOMETHING IN ME.

KURO...
I'D RATHER...
...BE ALONE...
I CAN'T LET IT.
I CAN'T LET IT.
I'D RATHER FACE DAYS THAT ARE PIERCING COLD...
...SO I DON'T ALLOW MYSELF ANY FALSE HOPES.
JUST LIKE IT ALWAYS WAS......
I DON'T WANT...ANY MORE THAN THAT......
KUROTO—...
WHEN I MET YOU, KUROTO, YOU WERE REFUSING EVERYTHING AND EVERY-ONE AROUND YOU.
AND MAYBE, AT ITS ROOTS, THAT HASN'T CHANGED......

—MAYBE I CAN'T SAVE YOU AFTER ALL...
OR CHANGE YOU...
NOW THAT I'VE GOT YOU...
...THAT'S ALL I NEED...
—...I DON'T WANT IT.
I'M FINE.

—HUH?
...WHAT, NOW?
WHAT DO YOU MEAN, "HUH?"...
—~~
...DON'T SAY SUCH STUPID THINGS!
WHAT A RELIEF...
I WAS AFRAID YOU WERE GOING TO SAY YOU DON'T WANT ME AROUND, EITHER.
YOU'RE THE ONE WHO FORCED YOUR WAY INTO MY LIFE.

..."THAT TIME."
WHEN I WAS TRYING TO LEAVE, AND YOU'RE THE ONE WHO WOULDN'T LET ME-
—...YEAH...
I GUESS IT WOULD HAVE BEEN A LOT EASIER FOR YOU...
...IF I JUST LET YOU GO, THAT TIME......
...SO, FOR BETTER OR WORSE...
...I'M STUCK WITH YOU.
HEE HEE
...YEP!

YOU'RE STUCK WITH ME! THAT HAS SUCH A NICE RING TO IT.
I'LL TAKE CARE OF YOU FOREVER AND EVER! ♥
YOU DUMMY... THAT'S NOT WHAT I...
KUSHA (RUFFLE)
MEALS AND SNACKS
AND LAUNDRY TOO
GAAAH!
GYULI (SQUEEEZE)
YOU ARE SO CUUUTE, KUROTO. ♥
QUIT TALKING LIKE THAT, IT'S GROSS! LET ME GO!!
...EVEN IF YOU SAY YOU DON'T WANT ME TO, I'LL STAY BESIDE YOU FOR-EVER.
—YOU'RE AS STUB-BORN...
...AS WHEN I FIRST MET YOU...
...AND AS ADOR-ABLE...
...AND AS SAD.
—AT LEAST...

...YOU CAN LET ME CARRY HALF YOUR BURDENS.

I'LL STAY BESIDE YOU, AND SEE THE SAME SIGHTS.

WE'LL WALK, SHOULDER TO SHOULDER...

...TO THE SAME PLACES...

NOW THAT I HAVE THE STRENGTH TO DO THAT.
GO (SOCK)
...LET ME GO AL-READY!!
BIKU (STARTLE)
...HEE-HEE.
SENSHIROU...
YOU'RE FINALLY OFF YOUR ROCKER...
ALL RIGHT! WHY DON'T I CHANGE INTO MY GEAR AND COME JOIN YOU.
LET'S HAVE OUR-SELVES A MATCH...
...KUROTO!

MOOOM! I'M DONE CLEANING THE BATH.
MOM?
SHE'S WATERING THE PLANTS...
...OUT ON THE BALCONY WITH LIA.
OH, OKAY.
MASAMUNE, CAN YOU STAY OVER TONIGHT?
SURE, I CAN.
IT'S A LITTLE DANGEROUS WITH THE INCIDENTS IN UENO PARK, SO TAKA-SHIRO-SAMA THOUGHT I SHOULD—
I SEE.
YEAH.

THESE INCIDENTS... ALONG WITH WHAT HAPPENED TO YAMATO, IT'S CAUSING SOME UPROAR AT ENJU.
THEY'RE SAYING IT'S A CURSE OR SOMETHING...
I GUESS KIDS WOULD THINK THAT, WHEN THREE STUDENTS AT THE SAME SCHOOL HAVE DIED.
THOUGH I DON'T WATCH THE NEWS SO I DON'T REALLY KNOW—
PESHI (WHACK)
THAT'S NOTHING TO BRAG ABOUT!
OW!
SASU (RUB) SASU
WELL, I HAVE TO STAY WITH MY MOM SOMETIMES.
BUT IF YOU WERE COMING, SAIRI...
...IT WOULD HAVE BEEN NICE IF YOU BROUGHT YUKI-KUN TOO.
THAT'D MAKE MOM REALLY HAPPY.
NO...
ACTUALLY, HE WANTED TO COME ALONG.
—OH, GEEZ, THAT'S KIND OF SELFISH.
YUKI-KUN HAS HIS OWN STUFF TO WORRY ABOUT...

BUT I TOLD HIM NOT TO.
POOON (BOUNCE)
ポーン
WUFF!
タタッ
TATA (DASH)
SHU (WHOOSH)

YOU LOOK A LITTLE DOWN...
...YUKI.
LUKA.
OH, NO, I'M FINE.
BUT YOU WERE GIVING OFF AN AIR OF WORRY.
I-I WAS? ...AM I THAT EASY TO READ...
—...I'VE JUST BEEN A LITTLE CONCERNED ABOUT KAYAKO-SAN...
AND SOMETHING'S HAPPENED IN UENO PARK, RIGHT?
TSUKUMO-KUN AND THE OTHERS WENT TO INVESTIGATE.
I JUST HOPE IT DOESN'T TURN INTO SOMETHING WORSE...
......

—AND ON TOP OF THAT...
...SAIRI-SAN...
WHAT DID HE DO?
......
...ACTUALLY, WHEN SAIRI-SAN CAME TO GET TSUKUMO-KUN AND THE OTHERS...
...HE SAID HE WOULD ALSO BE VISITING KAYAKO-SAN, AND I WANTED TO GO TOO.
BUT...
NO.
YOU'RE NOT COMING.
—HE SAID THAT?
YEAH...
I REMEMBERED THE FIRST TIME I MET HIM.
THOSE EYES OF HIS...
...LIKE NO ONE ELSE'S, SO COLD AND DISTANT—...
......YUKI.
DON'T THINK... ABOUT HIM ANYMORE.
NO MATTER HOW HARD YOU TRY TO UNDER-STAND HIM, IT'LL ONLY BE PAINFUL FOR YOU...

...WHY DO YOU SAY THAT?
DOES IT HAVE TO DO WITH A PREVIOUS LIFE?
......
YOU TOLD ME THAT THE ZWEILT CAN NEVER HATE ME...
BUT......
SAIRI-SAN—
IT FEELS LIKE HE DOES HATE ME.
...THAT!
UON! (WHINE!)
HE HE (PANT)
PON (POOF)

MASTER!
YUK-KIEEEE!
YOU'RE UNHAPPY?
SODOM!
I'M OKAY, REALLY! I'M HAPPY.
WHAT ABOUT MASTER?
REALLY TRULY?
UH-HUH.
YES... I'M FINE.
WHEW!
...OH, GOOD!
...BUT, BUT, HOTTSU AND TSUKKU DIDN'T LOOK SO GOOD.
HE MEANS TSUKUMO.
WHAT?
WOW. YOU EVEN NOTICED THAT, SODOM?
YEAH. AND HOTTSU GAVE SODOM SOME MEAT! HE SAID "I'M NOT HUNGRY."
......
AND, AND, AND TSUKKU...
WHEN SODOM WAS GOING ON A MIDNIGHT WALK, TSUKKU WAS AT THE "FIRING RANGE"—
THE FIRING RANGE?
MOYA (WOOOSH)
モヤモヤ
MOYA

DON (BLAM)
DON
DON
DON
DON
DON
HARARI (FLUTTER)
WHOOOA! COOL!!
YOU MADE A HOLE IN THE SHAPE OF A HEART!♬
...SODOM, YOU WERE IN HERE?
YESSIR!
...TAKING A WALK?
WHATCHA DOIN', TSUKKU?
...I... COULDN'T SLEEP.

—I KNOW. SODOM, WHY DON'T YOU SLEEP WITH ME?
I MISS SLEEPING NEXT TO SOMEONE......
ZZZZ...
すー
...THAT'S HOW IT WENT.
SODOM HELPED!
R-RIGHT...
BECAUSE TSUKUMO-KUN DOES SLEEP NEXT TO TOOKO-CHAN A LOT...
—IT'S TRUE, HOTSUMA-KUN AND TSUKUMO-KUN HAVEN'T QUITE BEEN THEMSELVES...
IT MUST BE BECAUSE THEIR PARTNERS SHUUSEI-KUN AND TOOKO-CHAN...
...ARE AWAY ON THE CLASS TRIP.
THAT'S ALL?
ER—
THEY'RE ACTING LIKE THAT JUST BECAUSE THEIR COLLEAGUES ARE AWAY?
IS THAT WHAT YOU WERE THINKING?
NO... UM...
...TO THE ZWEILT, THEIR PARTNER ISN'T JUST A PROFESSIONAL COLLEAGUE...
"PARTNER" MEANS "SOMEONE VERY DEAR" TO THEM.
...IRREPLACEABLE, BOUND BY A CONNECTION DEEPER THAN ANYTHING—A PERSON WHO'S VERY, VERY DEAR.

DEAR......
RIGHT... IT MEANS A PERSON YOU LOVE.
THE PERSON TO WHOM YOU WANT TO BE AS KIND AS YOU CAN BE.
THE ONE YOU WANT TO STAY WITH FOREVER AND EVER, AND...
...THE PERSON YOU WANT TO PROTECT, NO MATTER WHAT IT TAKES... I THINK.
OOH. THAT'S KINDA NEAT!
THE ZWEILT REALLY ARE COMPLICATED...
NO.
...OR MAYBE IT'S BETTER TO SAY I DIDN'T TRY TO.
...IS THAT TOO...
I FEEL LIKE I UNDERSTAND A LITTLE ABOUT THE WAY THEIR CONNECTIONS ARE......
...YOU DIDN'T UNDERSTAND BEFORE?
I COULD NEVER THINK OF ANYTHING BUT YOU.

...WHAT IT MEANS TO HAVE SOMEONE "DEAR"...?
YUKI.
WHAT WE WERE SPEAKING OF BEFORE...
Y-YES?
THE ONE HE HATES ISN'T YOU.
...IT'S ME.
WHEN HE TOLD YOU NOT TO COME, IT MUST HAVE BEEN BECAUSE HE DIDN'T WANT TO BE AROUND ME ANY MORE THAN NECESSARY.
HE HATES YOU...? ...BECAUSE YOU'RE A DURAS?
....I SUPPOSE SO.
...ANYWAY, YOU DON'T HAVE TO WORRY ABOUT IT.
I DON'T WANT YOU...
...TO TAKE ANY MORE BURDENS ONTO YOURSELF, YUKI......
—LUKA...
...IS WORRYING ABOUT ME—

I REALIZED IT A LITTLE WHILE AGO.

LUKA...

...DOESN'T ONLY WANT TO PROTECT ME FROM PHYSICAL HARM. HE WANTS TO PROTECT MY HEART TOO.

LIKE HE'S THERE TO WRAP ME UP AND KEEP ME FROM GETTING HURT...

—YES. I'VE DECIDED...

...TO GET MY MEMORIES BACK MYSELF.

WHEN MY MEMORIES COME BACK, EVERYTHING WILL MAKE SENSE.
BUT LUKA— I CAN'T TELL HIM... I'LL JUST MAKE HIM WORRY.
I'LL BE ABLE TO USE MY ABILITY AS THE LIGHT OF GOD PROPERLY...
...AND I'LL UNDERSTAND WHY SAIRI-SAN ACTS THAT WAY—...
TWILIGHT HALL REALLY IS HUGE... IT'S LIKE A MAZE...
AND THERE ARE A LOT OF ROOMS THAT AREN'T EVEN BEING USED.
IT FEELS LESS LIKE A MANSION THAN A CASTLE...
I'M GONNA GET LOST ANY MINUTE NOW...
IF I MADE MYSELF FORGET ABOUT LUKA AND EVERYONE ELSE...
...BECAUSE I WANTED TO RUN AWAY FROM THE MEMORY OF SOMETHING PAINFUL IN THE PAST...
...I CAN'T FORGIVE MYSELF FOR THAT......
—IF I DID SEAL AWAY MY OWN MEMORIES...
...ISN'T THAT LIKE "RUNNING AWAY"?

I CAN'T JUST LET SOMEONE ELSE TELL ME.
I HAVE TO REMEMBER FOR MY-SELF—
—IS WHAT I DECIDED...
...BUT I HAVEN'T BEEN ABLE...
...TO REMEMBER THE SLIGHT-EST LITTLE THING AT ALL......
THIS ISN'T GOING SO WELL...
IF I KEEP TRYING TO MAKE MYSELF REMEMBER I'LL JUST GET A HEADACHE...
......HM?
HUH... WAS THERE A DOOR HERE BEFORE...?
ALL THESE DOORS LOOK ALIKE...
GACHA (K-CHAK)
IT OPENED.
STAIRS—...?

TON (TMP)
AND ALL THE WAY AT THE END...
...A ROOM—
DOKIN (BADUM)
WHAT CAN THIS BE...
I'M SURE I'VE SEEN THIS BEFORE......
DOKIN
IT DEFINITELY LOOKS DIFFERENT FROM THE REST OF THE HOUSE...
IT'S LOCKED...
DOKIN
KACHA (OPEN)
OH!
IT OPENED.
DOKIN
GII (CREAK)

I KNOW THIS PLACE...
THIS PLACE—
I'VE BEEN IN THIS ROOM BEFORE...

RIGHT.
A DESK.
FOR SOME REASON...
...THAT DESK STICKS OUT IN MY MIND...
ON THE RIGHT...
THE BOTTOM DRAWER...
GOKU (GULP)
KARA (SLIDE)

AN OLD... WRITING PAD...?
PARA (FLIP)
PAGE: I AM REGRETTING IT. [...] ACT...
私は後悔している。
DOKIN (BADUM)
I AM REGRETTING IT.
TO THINK THIS SELFISH ACT OF MINE HAS BROUGHT SUCH CONSEQUENCES...
THE COST HAS BEEN TOO GREAT.

代償は
私は償えるだろうか…
もう　裏切れない
あのひとと…　倖せになることはできない
WITH THAT PERSON ...?
BETRAY...?
WHAT... IS THIS......
WHO COULD HAVE WRITTEN THIS ......?
PAGE: THE COST HAS [...] / I WONDER IF I CAN ATONE FOR THIS... / I CAN BETRAY NO MORE... / IT'S IMPOSSIBLE. TO BE HAPPY WITH THAT PERSON.

—I SEE...
SO IT DID TURN OUT TO BE A MURDER CASE.
YES... FROM THE CLOTHES YAMADA-KUN WAS WEARING, I COULD HEAR IT, FAINTLY...
A PAINED VOICE PLEADING "PLEASE DON'T KILL ME"...
THOUGH I COULDN'T GET ANYTHING FROM MASUDA-KUN'S BELONGINGS—
DO THE DURAS HAVE ANYTHING TO DO WITH IT?
SORRY, WE DON'T KNOW...
IF SHUUSEI WERE HERE, HE COULD PROBABLY TELL......
BUT JUST ONE WAS A MURDER— THE OTHER WAS A SUICIDE... RIGHT?
THEY DON'T HAVE TO BE CONNECTED JUST BECAUSE IT'S A RIDICULOUS COINCIDENCE.
—STILL.
TAKASHIRO DID DECIDE TO HAVE WORLD END LOOK INTO IT.
YEAH.
AND DEPENDING HOW IT GOES, HE MIGHT KEEP US ON THE CASE TOO.

I SAY BRING IT ON.
...OF COURSE...
...THERE'S THE BARRIER TO THINK OF, SO WE CAN'T JUST IGNORE IT.
—MY HEAD HURTS...
ZUKIN (THROB)
ズキン
ZUKIN
ズキン
I GUESS IT'S BECAUSE I'VE BEEN THINKING ABOUT IT FOR TOO LONG.
ZUKIN
ズキン
THAT ROOM, AND THE THINGS ON THAT LETTER PAD......
ZUKIN
ズキン
I FEEL LIKE I CAN ALMOST REMEMBER SOMETHING IMPORTANT...
ZUKIN
ズキン
BUT MY HEAD HURTS—
ガチャ
GACHA (OPEN)
EVERYONE...
...I HAVE SOME NEWS.
TACHIBANA-SAN...
IT'S NOT GOOD NEWS.
PLEASE, LISTEN TO ME CALMLY.

WH-WHAT DO YOU MEAN...?
SHUUSEI-KUN AND TOOKO-CHAN ARE INCOMMUNICADO ......!
OUR PEACEFUL "NORMAL LIFE" HAS COME TO AN END—

THE
BETRAYAL
KNOWS MY NAME

Story 45
THE TWO WHO DISAPPEARED

—WE SHOULD REACH KYOTO AROUND DAWN.
WE'VE BEEN TOLD...
...TO GO STRAIGHT TO THE MAIN FAMILY'S RESIDENCE, SO—
"THE MAIN BRANCH IN KYOTO"...... I'LL MEET THEM FOR THE FIRST TIME.
AND NOW...
...WE HAVE TO GO SEE THEM UNDER THESE CIRCUM-STANCES—...
WHAT DO YOU MEAN!? SHUUSEI-KUN AND TOOKO-CHAN ARE INCOM-MUNICADO...

THEY WERE ON THAT CLASS TRIP—
SO THEY MUST BE IN KYOTO NOW, RIGHT?
...ABOUT THAT.
BOTH OF THEM WERE TOLD TO MAKE AN APPEARANCE AT THE MAIN HOUSE IN KYOTO TONIGHT.
THEY WERE SUPPOSED TO BE THERE AT NINE-THIRTY...
...BUT APPARENTLY, THEY NEVER SHOWED UP.
THEY NEVER SHOWED UP—!?
THAT'S RIGHT.
NEITHER OF THEM ARE ANSWERING THEIR CELL PHONES.
WE CHECKED WITH THEIR TEACHER AT THE INN TOO...
...BUT THERE'S NO SIGN OF THEM THERE, EITHER......
—AND...
...WE STILL HAVEN'T HEARD FROM THEM.

THAT CAN'T BE RIGHT......
COULD IT BE DURAS?
WE DON'T KNOW...
ALL WE KNOW RIGHT NOW IS THAT THEY'RE INCOMMUNICADO.
YOU'LL HEAR MORE FROM THE COMMANDER.
HE'S HEADING HERE NOW—
KATSU (TAK)
KATSU
KATSU
COM-MANDER!
TAKA-SHIRO-SAMA!

IT LOOKS LIKE YOU'RE ALL HERE.

I'VE JUST RECEIVED A NEW REPORT.
IT SEEMS A PRIVATE HOME NOT FAR FROM THE GIOU MAIN HOUSE...
...TOOK IN THREE YOUNG WOMEN WHO WERE IN A STATE OF CONFUSION AND DISTRESS.

ONE, A JUNIOR COLLEGE STUDENT, WAS INJURED, THOUGH NOT SERIOUSLY, AND WAS TAKEN TO THE HOSPITAL.
BUT THE POINT IS THE OTHER TWO— I'M TOLD THEY WERE BOTH CLASSMATES OF TOOKO'S.
!!
TOOKO-CHAN'S...
WE'RE STILL INVESTIGATING, BUT THEY SAY...
...THEY WERE SUDDENLY ATTACKED BY A PSYCHOTIC MAN.

A PSYCHOTIC ......!?
APPARENTLY IT WAS A MAN DRESSED COMPLETELY IN BLACK.
AND THEN, THEY SAID, THEY WERE RESCUED BY SHUUSEI AND TOOKO—
BUT SINCE THEY WERE SO DESPERATE TO GET AWAY...
...THEY DON'T KNOW WHAT HAPPENED TO SHUUSEI AND TOOKO AFTER THAT.
WHAT THE HELL'S THAT MEAN— A PSYCHO!?
THERE'S GOTTA BE A BETTER LEAD THAN THAT!
—I ORDERED AN INVESTIGATION AT THE SPOT WHERE THE GIRLS SAID THEY WERE AT-TACKED.
IT'S A PLACE WHERE NOT MANY PEOPLE COME BY... A RUN-DOWN NEIGHBORHOOD.
AND LARGE BLOODSTAINS WERE FOUND.
! DOES THAT MEAN...
...SHUUSEI-KUN AND TOOKO-CHAN WERE HURT...?
IT COULD, BUT...
...IF THAT "PSYCHOTIC MAN" OR WHATEVER WAS JUST A HUMAN, THOSE TWO COULDN'T HAVE LOST TO HIM...

——......IT'S THE DURAS.
REIGA HAS FINALLY...
...MADE HIS MOVE.

REIGA HAS MADE HIS MOVE.
—WHAT THE HELL...
...IS GOING ON HERE?
SHUUSEI......
—CURRENTLY, WORLD END IS CONCENTRATING ON THE MOUN-TAINS AROUND SAGANO...
...IN THE SEARCH FOR SHUUSEI AND TOOKO.
UP...IN THE MOUNTAINS?
YES. THE SCENE OF THE CRIME IS NEAR THE WAY UP TO THE MOUNTAINS.
ZWEILT, WHEN THEY FIGHT...
...GENERALLY CHOOSE A DESERTED PLACE, SO AS TO AVOID BEING SEEN BY OR INJURING BY-STANDERS.

...IF THERE ARE MOUNTAINS NEARBY...
...THEY PROBABLY TRIED TO DRAW THEIR OPPONENT THAT WAY FIRST.
....
......TAKA-SHIRO.
I SURE HOPE...
...YOU'RE NOT THINKIN' OF LEAVIN' ME OFF THE SEARCH TEAM.
I'LL TELL YOU RIGHT NOW, I'M PERFECTLY CALM.
I'M NOT GONNA LET IT GET TO ME AND JUST GO RUNNIN' OFF AFTER SOMETHING, LIKE THAT ONE TIME.

I...
...CAN FIND SHUUSEI.
HOTSUMA.
HOW ARE THOSE PEOPLE GONNA FIND ANYTHING IN THE MOUNTAINS WHEN THEY GOT NOTHING TO GO ON?
BUT US— ...THE ZWEILT...
DON'T...
...EVER DOUBT.
WE CAN SENSE OUR PARTNERS.
IF OUR FEELINGS FOR THEM ARE STRONG ENOUGH...
I CAN FIND HIM.
SO LET ME GO!

TAKASHIRO-SAMA—
I CAN TOO!
I WILL FIND TOOKO-CHAN! SIR, PLEASE LET ME GO!
M...ME TOO!
ESPECIALLY IF THEY'VE BEEN HURT— I CAN HELP!
TAKASHIRO!
TAKASHIRO-SAMA...!
....
...I WAS PLANNING...
...TO PUT YOU ON THE SEARCH TO BEGIN WITH.
THAT IS, AFTER I DETERMINED WHETHER YOU WOULD BE ABLE TO ACT CALMLY.

...VERY WELL.
THE THREE OF YOU HAVE PERMISSION TO GO TO KYOTO...
...AND JOIN THE SEARCH FOR SHUUSEI AND TOOKO—
......TOOKO-CHAN—
ZAA (RUSTLE)
WHERE ARE YOU?
ANSWER ME.
TOOKO-CHAN......!

—THE THREE OF YOU, HOTSUMA, TSUKUMO, AND YUKI...
...HAVE PERMISSION TO JOIN THE SEARCH.
TAKASHIRO-SAMA, LET US—
NO.
I CAN'T LEAVE TOKYO UNMANNED AT THIS POINT.
KUROTO AND SENSHIROU, SAIRI AND LIA...
I NEED YOU TO STAY HERE AND INVESTIGATE THE UENO PARK CASES.
...LUKA, YOU GO WITH THEM AS WELL. TAKE CARE OF YUKI.
I WILL.
UNDER-STOOD?
......YES, SIR...

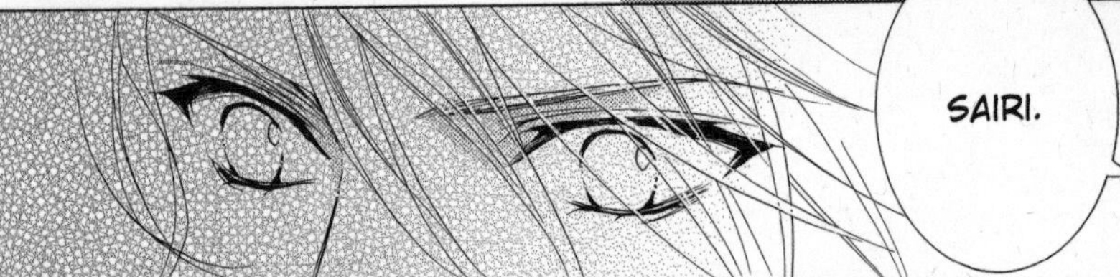

WHERE... ARE YOU GOING?

LIA, WEREN'T YOU ASLEEP?

...I'M GOING TO TALK TO TAKASHIRO-SAMA—

...I WANT TO SEE IF I CAN GET HIM TO LET ME GO TO KYOTO TOO.

WHY...?
BECAUSE I'M WORRIED, OF COURSE.
SHUUSEI AND TOOKO-CHAN MIGHT BE IN DANGER...
AND THE MORE PEOPLE SEARCHING, THE BET-TER......
THAT'S NOT TRUE......!
YOU'RE LYING!
YOU'RE JUST THINKING OF GOING TO YUKI-SAMA'S SIDE AND PROTECTING HIM YOURSELF, AREN'T YOU ...!?

......
...LIA, THAT'S NOT IT.
I REALLY DO WANT TO GO SEARCH FOR SHUUSEI AND TOOKO-CHAN......
I KNOW THAT'S IMPORTANT TOO—...
BUT, SAIRI, ISN'T PROTECTING YUKI MORE IMPORTANT TO YOU THAN ANYTHING...?
...DIDN'T YOU DECIDE TO DISTANCE YOURSELF FROM HIM?
—... DON'T...
DON'T GO......
YUKI WILL BE FINE EVEN IF YOU'RE NOT THERE...
HE'LL HAVE HOTSUMA AND TSUU-KUN...
......AND LUKA WITH HIM.
LIA......
PLEASE, SAIRI.
IT'S BETTER THAT WAY.
...IF YOU—

IF YOU STAY BY HIS SIDE...
...IT'LL BREAK YOU!......
—IT FEELS LIKE...
...I'M ABOUT TO GO MAD.

THOUGH I'D RATHER LOSE MY SANITY IF I COULD.
......ANY MAN...
AND BE DONE WITH HUMAN EMO-TIONS.
...WOULD HAVE TO GIVE IN, I THINK...
...WITH A PRETTY GIRL LIKE YOU CLINGING TO HIM, LIA......
....
...I DON'T CARE ABOUT JUST ANY MAN.
IF IT DOESN'T REACH SAIRI, AND ONLY SAIRI...
...THEN THERE'S NO POINT......
—...IT'S NO GOOD.

I CAN'T GET THROUGH TO HER......
TSU-KUMO-KUN?
I THOUGHT, SINCE WE'RE GETTING CLOSER...
...MAYBE I COULD REACH TOOKO-CHAN TELEPATHI-CALLY...
BUT I CAN'T PICK UP A SINGLE THING FROM HER...
AND THAT NEVER HAPPENS......
I CAN ALWAYS PICK UP HER VOICE.
WHAT DO WE DO— IF I CAN'T HEAR ANY-THING, THAT MEANS......
...SHE'S IN A STATE WHERE SHE CAN'T TALK TO ME, AND THAT MEANS...
SHE'S BEING HELD SOMEWHERE, OR SHE'S UNCON-SCIOUS......
OR, THE WORST—
ZOKU (CHILL)

THEY'RE OKAY. THEY HAVE TO BE OKAY!!
...HOTSU-MA...
TSU-KUMO!
QUIT THINKIN' CRAP LIKE THAT!
...YOU LOVE TOOKO, RIGHT? YOU DO!
YOU GUYS'RE ALWAYS BEIN' SO CLINGY IT'S ANNOYING!
HOTSUMA-KUN...
THAT WAS SUDDEN...
...Y-YEAH, I ADORE HER.
THEN QUIT RELYIN' ON YOUR EAR AND JUST TRY TO FEEL HER! DON'T GET ALL MOPEY!
...WITH-OUT USING MY EAR...
DO THE ZWEILT HAVE THAT KIND OF ABILITY TOO?
IT'S NOT AN ABILITY, IT'S MORE LIKE INTUITION. LIKE A SIXTH SENSE KIND OF THING.
...THAT'S WHAT SHUUSEI TOLD ME A WHILE BACK.
—HE WAS ALWAYS ABLE TO READ ME LIKE A BOOK, Y'KNOW.
AND HE'D KNOW RIGHT WHERE I WAS...... IT WAS PRETTY WEIRD.

WASN'T HE...JUST USING HIS "EYE OF GOD" THEN?
THAT'S WHAT I THOUGHT AT FIRST TOO, BUT HE SAID HE WASN'T—
OUR SYNC RATE AS PARTNERS IS PRETTY HIGH...
...SO WE CAN SENSE EACH OTHER EVEN WHEN WE'RE APART...
IT'S JUST A THING WE USED TO DO ALL THE TIME WAY BACK WHEN THAT WE KINDA FORGOT ABOUT.
...YEAH...... YOU'RE RIGHT.
MAYBE... I HAVE BEEN RELYING TOO MUCH ON MY "EAR OF GOD" ABILITY......
THANKS, HOTSUMA. I FEEL A LITTLE BETTER NOW.
...HOTSUMA-KUN, YOU'RE... I THINK...
UM, WHAT DO YOU CALL IT...
I THINK PEOPLE USE IT A LOT ABOUT TAKASHIRO-SAN AND LUKA—
OH, YEAH! YOU'RE "DEPENDABLE"!!
OHH! YEAAAH, HE IS!
SOMEHOW YOU'RE CALMER THAN USUAL!
BUT YOU STILL HAVE PLENTY OF YOUR UNFOUNDED SELF-CONFIDENCE ♪
I GUESS BEING THE DUMB, LOUD ONE HAS ITS USES TOO.
CHUCKLE
ARE YOU PEOPLE COMPLIMENTIN' OR CRITICIZIN' ME!?

—......
THE REASON I CAN STAY CALM IS...
...'COS HE SAID......
DON'T LOSE SIGHT OF YOURSELF.
IF YOU CAN DO THAT, THEN I WILL COME BACK TO YOU...
SHUUSEI... YOU COULDN'T HAVE JUST SAID THOSE THINGS...
...BECAUSE YOU KNEW SOMETHING LIKE THIS WOULD HAPPEN...
—COME BACK.
YOU GOTTA.
YOU PROM-ISED...
SHUUSEI—
ZA CKTCHD

TOTSU (THUMP)
HFF
HFF
GAKU (BUCKLE)
NGH...
COUGH
BOTO (DRIP)
...... IT'S NO GOOD... I CAN'T RUN ANYMORE.
I'VE LOST TOO MUCH BLOOD—...

...I WONDER IF TOOKO GOT AWAY SAFELY......
...HOTSUMA—...
—TOO MUCH BLOOD ...
HFF
...I'M NOT GOING TO MAKE IT......
Story 45 · END

The
Betrayal
knows my name

Story 46
WOOF!
WOOF! WOOF!
ZAAAA (SSSHH)
WOOF!
WOOF!
WOOF!

SOMEBODY HELP...

YUKI-CHAN...

TSUKUMO...

HOTSUMA......

Story 46

A DARK NIGHT

ABOUT EIGHT HOURS AGO—
KYOTO
TOOKO'S LATE...
—HUH ...?
NEWS
Latest Headlines
Murder by a vampire!? Body found drained of blood.
"MURDER BY A VAMPIRE"—
WHAT IS THAT ABOUT...?

A YOUNG WOMAN'S BODY WAS FOUND THIS MORNING IN KYOTO.
AUTHORITIES DISCOVERED THAT NOT A SINGLE DROP OF BLOOD REMAINED IN THE BODY...
THERE ARE TWO HOLES IN THE NECK, THROUGH WHICH IT APPEARS THE BLOOD WAS DRAINED......
IS THIS BIZARRE CRIME THE ACT OF A DERANGED MANIAC, OR—...
SHUU-SEI!
SORRY...
...I'M SO LATE!
HFF! HFF!
YOU DIDN'T HAVE TO RUSH LIKE THAT.
B-BUT THE MAIN FAMILY... THEY'RE SUCH STICKLERS ABOUT TIME.
IT'S ALL RIGHT. WE'LL MAKE IT BY 9:30.
I'VE GOT A CAB WAITING.
I'M REALLY SORRY. IT TOOK ME LONGER THAN I THOUGHT TO SNEAK OUT WITHOUT MY FRIENDS NOTICING...
SNEAK OUT?
BUT WE HAVE PERMISSION FROM THE TEACHER AND EVERYTHING. THERE'S NO REASON FOR SNEAKING.
OH— WELL, UM...
THE THING IS—

PACHI
THEY THINK YOU AND I ARE GOING OUT?
THERE ARE REALLY RUMORS LIKE THAT GOING AROUND?
YEAH.
I MEAN, PEOPLE SEE US TOGETHER A LOT, RIGHT?
"OH, THEY MUST BE PRETTY CLOSE," EVERYONE THINKS...
...AND LATELY THEY'VE STARTED SUSPECTING... YOU KNOW.
ON TOP OF THAT, IF PEOPLE NOTICED THAT WE WERE LEAVING THE INN TOGETHER AT THIS TIME OF NIGHT...
I DON'T EVEN WANT TO THINK ABOUT IT.
IT'S A PRETTY SPECIAL OCCASION THAT WE GOT
I HAD NO IDEA...
I SHOULD BE MORE CAREFUL HOW I ACT AROUND YOU.
OH, NO, DON'T WORRY ABOUT IT!
IT'S NOT YOUR FAULT, SHUUSEI!
BUT...
IT CAN'T BE GOOD FOR YOU, HAVING THAT SORT OF RUMOR...

WHEN I GET A CHANCE, I'LL TRY TO CLEAR UP THE MISUNDERSTANDING MYSELF.
OH...OKAY. THANKS. THAT WOULD HELP...
......
—...YEAH.
...SO...
...HAVING PEOPLE SAY THAT YOU AND I ARE GOING OUT... THAT BOTHERS YOU, SHUUSEI?
IF— I MEAN... IF WE...... MANAGE TO SURVIVE AGAIN...... THEN—
...TOOKO?
THEN OUR NEXT MISSION WILL BE "KEEPING THE BLOOD STRONG"... WON'T IT?
THAT'S THE CONVENTION...

HOUSE GIOU
THOSE BORN OF THE TEN DIVINE HOUSES, OF WHICH GIOU IS THE MAIN BRANCH...
HOUSE SHIN-MEI
HOUSE MURA-SAME
HOUSE RENJOU
HOUSE USUI
HOUSE HOURAI
HOUSE FURU-ORI
HOUSE OTONA
HOUSE SHIKIBE
HOUSE REIZEN
...MUST TAKE A SPOUSE FROM ANOTHER ONE OF THE TEN—
THE ZWEILT ARE ALWAYS REBORN
WITHIN ONE OF THE TEN DIVINE HOUSES.
SO, TO MAIN-TAIN THE STRENGTH OF THE BLOOD
...AND TO CREATE "VESSELS" FOR THE ZWEILT OF THE FUTURE—

—AND A MARRIAGE OF TWO ZWEILT IS EVEN MORE PREFERABLE...
FOR LONG CENTURIES...
...THAT CRUELTY HAS BEEN FORCED ON US—
...ON WOMEN, ESPECIALLY.
N-NO, IT ISN'T CRUEL.
IT'S AN IMPORTANT DUTY THAT FALLS TO ALL OF US, BOTH MEN AND WOMEN...
......I WONDER IF...
...IN THIS LIFE, MAYBE...
...YOU'LL BE MY HUSBAND.

ACK!
UH, NEVER MIND...
...TOOKO, WOULD YOU LIKE TO BE MY BRIDE?
UH HEY, C'MON-
I-I WAS JUST SAYING, IF YOU WOULDN'T MIND IT......
I-I MEAN—
SENSHIROU-SAN HAS TSUBAKI-SAN...
AND SAIRI-KUN HAS LIA, RIGHT?
AND HOTSUMA AND KUROTO ARE BOTH YOUNGER THAN ME, SO—...
THAT'S TRUE.
IT WOULD ONLY BE NATURAL FOR THE MAIN BRANCH TO APPROVE ME AS A MATCH FOR YOU.
—~~~...
A-ACTU-ALLY...
BEFORE WE LEFT, TSUKUMO SAID TO ME...
—TOOKO-CHAN...
...WHEN THE WAR IS OVER THIS TIME, ARE YOU GOING TO MARRY SHUUSEI?

MARRY!?
WH-WH-WHERE DID THAT COME FROM!!?
GATA (CLUNK)
YOU DIDN'T KNOW? THERE'S A RUMOR GOING AROUND AT SCHOOL THAT YOU AND SHUUSEI ARE GOING OUT.
A RU...
SO... YOU HEARD THAT TOO, HUH......
WELL, I DO HAVE A PRETTY GOOD EAR.
OBVIOUSLY... ......IT'S JUST A RUMOR.
YEAH... I KNOW.
BUT THE FUTURE MIGHT BE CLOSER THAN WE THINK...
SINCE I HEARD THAT RUMOR...
...IT FELT LIKE SOMETHING THAT WAS ALWAYS VAGUE AND FAR-OFF...
...SUDDENLY CONFRONTED ME WITH ITS REALITY......

...SORRY.
IT'S STUPID TO BE THINKING ABOUT THAT STUFF NOW...
IT'LL JUST MAKE YOU UPSET, WON'T IT, TOOKO-CHAN—...
—AND I...
...HAD NO IDEA...
...WHAT TO SAY TO THAT...
....
...I WONDER WHY...
...THE PIECES...
...NEVER QUITE FIT PERFECTLY...
...WELL...
...TSUKUMO AND I AREN'T THE ONLY ONES LIKE THAT......
...COME TO THINK OF IT, NO MATTER THE ERA...
...YOU TWO ARE ALWAYS SIBLINGS.

...THE ZWEILT HAVE NOTHING BUT TROUBLE WITH THESE THINGS.
FAMILY...
FRIENDS......
...LOVERS......
WE CAN'T...
...REACH THEM—
...MAYBE...
...THE GODS DON'T WANT US...
...TO BE BLINDED BY THE LIGHT OF HAPPINESS ...?

...WANT TO WALK A BIT, TOOKO?
COULD YOU STOP UP THERE, PLEASE?
HUH? YEAH, SURE.
HAHH HAHH HAHH,
HAHH,
HAHH,
HFF

WOW!
THE MOON IS SO PRETTY!
IT IS NICE TO TAKE A LITTLE WALK LIKE THIS. ♪
...TOOKO.
I WANTED TO TALK SOME MORE ABOUT THAT...
......OKAY.
I THINK IT'S POSSIBLE THAT...
...THAT WITH THIS LIFETIME, WE MIGHT NOT NEED THAT "CONVENTION" ANYMORE.
ZAA (RUSTLE)

—NOT...
...NEED IT ANYMORE ......?
YEAH.
BECAUSE *THAT*...
...WAS ESTABLISHED ON THE PREMISE THAT THE WAR IS GOING TO *CONTINUE*.
BUT...
...THE WAR AGAINST REIGA...

...MUST COME TO AN END IN THIS LIFETIME.
...THAT'S WHAT I THINK.
THOUGH I DON'T KNOW WHAT SHAPE THAT END WILL TAKE.

OF COURSE, TAKASHIRO-SAMA MUST HAVE ALWAYS BEEN FIGHTING WITH THE AIM OF ENDING IT IN MIND...
...BUT THIS TIME, FOR BETTER OR WORSE, IS *DIFFERENT*......
DIFFERENT......
DO YOU... SENSE SOMETHING...?
—ANYWAY...
WHEN THE WAR IS OVER, THERE WILL BE NO MORE NEED FOR THE ZWEILT TO BE REINCARNATED.
AND THAT CONVENTION WON'T HAVE TO CONTINUE, EITHER.
—I-I NEVER...
...EVEN THOUGHT ABOUT IT...
THAT IT COULD *END*......
I KNOW...
THE OTHERS PROBABLY HAVEN'T, EITHER—
AT SOME POINT THE ZWEILT LOST HOLD OF THE IDEA THAT IT'S SUPPOSED TO "END."
THIS IS OUR INESCAPABLE FATE, WE KEEP THINKING—
THAT'S HOW LONG THIS WAR AGAINST REIGA HAS GONE ON. TOO LONG.

...BUT...
...I THINK...
...WE SHOULD HAVE MORE OF A WILL TO FIGHT AGAINST THINGS LIKE FATE AND DESTINY.
BE-CAUSE...
...YUKI SAID...
WHEN WE PUT AN END TO THIS WAR...
...HE WANTS TO SET US FREE—...

YUKI-CHAN.

...YEAH.
YOU'RE RIGHT.
IT IS GOING TO END.

WE'LL PROTECT THE THINGS WE CHERISH, THE PEOPLE WHO ARE IMPORTANT TO US...

AND WE WILL PUT AN END TO IT.

IF YUKI-CHAN IS HERE FOR US—

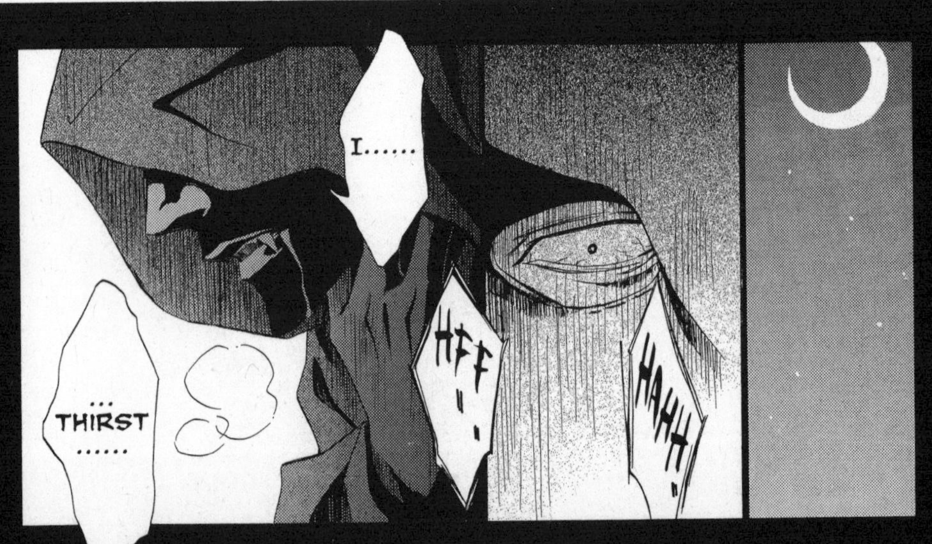

....
...SHUUSEI?
PIKU (TWITCH)
—WHY DON'T YOU JUST COME OUT?
I KNOW YOU'RE OVER THERE.
HUH?
WH-WHAT?
AH...
AAAAAHH!!
HYOKO (POP)
...HIII!
WE GOT CAUGHT, HUH?
ETSUKO!
SAYAKA! WHAT ARE YOU...

ER-
SORRY... SHUUSEI... UM, THESE ARE MY CLASSMATES—
I THOUGHT SO. THERE WAS A TAXI FOLLOWING US THE WHOLE WAY...
......
WHAT!? OH—
THAT'S WHY WE GOT OUT OF THE CAR!?
SO, THIS IS WHAT YOU SNUCK OUT OF THE INN FOR!
YOU THINK WE'LL LET YOU HAVE ALL THE FUN...
...DRAGGING THE PRINCE OUT TO A DESERTED PLACE LIKE THIS?
OH HOH HOH!
....
GEEZ, YOU TWO!
WHAT D'YOU THINK YOU'RE DOING!?
YOU BETTER EXPLAIN YOURSELF, TOOKO!
YOU TWO HAVE SOME NERVE FOR BUSTED SPIES...
... TOOKO...
...WOULD IT BE ALL RIGHT IF I EXPLAIN?
OOH, USUI-KUN, TAKING THE INITIATIVE!?
MY EYES! HIS CUTENESS IS DAZZLING!
THANK YOU, SHUUSEI, I'D APPRECIATE THAT......

MOMENTS LATER.

WHOOOA... YOU'RE A DISTANT COUSIN OF TOOKO'S!?
NO WAY! WHO'DVE THUNK?

YOU SHOULD'VE JUST SAID SO!
YOU GET IT NOW?
ANYWAY, TONIGHT, OUR RELATIVES ARE MAKING US VISIT THEM. THAT'S ALL!
—...
I'M PRETTY SURE I DID.
OH. DID YOU?
THEY LIVE AROUND HERE? THERE'S, LIKE, NOTHING.
I-IT'S IN THE MOUN-TAINS......
ZAWA (RUSTLE)
.........?
—YOU TWO...
...SHOULD GET BACK TO THE INN NOW.

Story 46 · END

THE
BETRAYAL
KNOWS MY NAME

Story 47

GASHAN (CLANK)
NO...
GET AWAY FROM ME!!
H-HELP ME...!!
KOTSU (TOK)
NIYA (GRIN)
ZOKU (FREEZE)

EEEEEEEK!!!
!!
SCREAMING—!!?
DA (DASH)
TOOKO!!
RIGHT!
¿HUH?
WH-WHAT!?
HEY... TOOKO! YOU'RE GOING AFTER IT!?

WE'LL BE RIGHT BACK!

YOU TWO STAY HERE!

AND DON'T MOVE!!

I HAVE A BAD FEELING ABOUT THIS...!

COULD YOU TELL WHERE THE SCREAM CAME FROM?

YEAH!

Story 47
Human? or Demon?
ギロリ
GIRORI (GLARE)

WHA...!? IS HE DRINKING HER BLOOD ...!?
Latest Headlines
Murder by a vampire!? Bod
found drained of blood.
COULD THAT...
...HAVE BEEN THIS GUY...!?
—CRY CROW.
POU (GLOW)
KYUN (PWIP)
DIOMEDES!!
KYUN
KYUPA (VWISH)
DO (BAM)
DO
DO
DO
DO

TAN (TMP)
VN (VMM)
IS HE A DURAS!?
NO...
I'M SENSING HUMAN PRES- ENCE.
ARE YOU ALL RIGHT!? HOLD ON!
UGH...
DON (BOOM)
HE'S UNDER DEMONIC POSSES- SION.
DO (WHOOM)
BA (JUMP)
WE HAVE TO EXORCISE HIM FIRST.
WE CAN'T DO ANYTHING WITH- OUT GETTING THE DURAS OUT OF THIS PERSON'S BODY!!

KYUOOOO (SHOOOOM)
EON!
FIGHT ME!
PHYSICALLY, THAT'S A HUMAN BEING.
I CAN'T USE LETHAL FORCE!!
GIN (CLANG)
GIN
GAKIN (KASHING)
FIRST BAR-RIER!
PHAEROS.
POU
ELCAT.
SEPAL.
SHUSE
POU (GLOW)

AYNTH.
!!
GI (GLANCE)
...I ISOLATE THIS SPACE—
NGH...!
BACHI
IN THE NAME OF THE ALMIGHTY, RULER OF WORLDS, MASTER OF THE FLOW OF TIME...
BYU (VWOOSH)
HE'S FAST!!
I DON'T HAVE A CHANCE TO PUT UP THE BARRIER!!

ZUGYA
(SWOOSH)
DO
(WHANG)
SORRY, SHUUSEI.
I LET MY GUARD DOWN.
!?

HYAAAAA!
DO
(ZISH)
DOGAA
(CRASH)
GAGIIN
(CLANNNG)

GIGIGI (STRAINING)
I RELEASE YOU!!
SHUUSE!! NOW!!
BISHI (SKISH)
BISHI
BISHI

POU (GLOW)
ZAZAZAZA (SKIDDD)
IS IT OUT...!?
JAKIN (KSHANG)
JAKI
JAKIN
SHUU (FSSH)

SHUUU

...THE DURAS...

...WON'T COME OUT ...!?

WHAT'S GOING ON!?

THERE'S DEFINITELY A HUMAN PRESENCE, BUT...

HE'S NOT "POS-SESSED"...

HE ACTUALLY IS A DURAS!?

!!
SUU (WSSH)
スウ
HE JUST WALKED THROUGH THE CAGE OF BINDING!?
...YOU CAN'T BE A DURAS ...!!
IF YOU WERE, YOU COULD NEVER PULL OFF A TRICK LIKE WALKING THROUGH THE BARS OF A CAGE OF BINDING!

AND YET—
...HOW CAN HE BE HUMAN—?
WHAT ON EARTH IS HE...!?
WITH THAT RIDICULOUS LEVEL OF POWER...
バタバタ
BATA (RUN)
BATA
TOOKO!?
WE HEARD ALL THIS NOISE AND...
EEP...!?
!!
DAMN ...!

GIRO (STARE)
BLOOD.....
NO...!
ETSU-KO—
GO (ZOOM)
RUN....!!
DO (BOOM)

ZAZA (SKID)
!?
......ARE YOU ALL RIGHT?
USUI-KUN...! TH-THANK YOU...
...NGH......
USUI-KUN!? WH-WHAT'S WRONG!?
EEEK!
YURA (WOBBLE)
YOU...
YOU'RE BLEEDING ......!!

KA (FLASH)
DOGO (KASHOOM)
ZA (KTCH)
TOOKO!
USUI-KUN'S HURT!!
WHAT'S HAPPENING...!?
ETSUKO! SAYAKA! FOR NOW—
JUST TAKE THAT WOMAN AND GET AWAY FROM HERE! QUICKLY!!
HUH?
B-BUT TOOKO, WHAT ABOUT YOU AND USUI-KUN!?
WE'LL BE OKAY!
GET HER TO A HOSPITAL...
OR A HOUSE! OR ANYTHING!
JUST GET OUT OF HERE!!

WE'LL GET HELP!
...O...
OKAY.
HAHH
HAHH
...BLOOOOOD!...
SO...
...THIR...STY...
CRY CROW—DIOMEDES.
KYUOOO (SHOOOM)
SHUUSEI, ARE YOU HURT BADLY ...!?
I THINK...
...MY LEFT ARM'S OUT OF PLAY......

WHAT DO WE DO?

IS THIS A HUMAN?
OR A DURAS?
BA (LUNGE)
WHAT DO WE DO!?
GO (ZHOOM)
JIJI (FLICKER)
—SO.

HOW IS THE BARRIER SITUATION?
LUZÉ.
IT IS QUITE SOLID, HAVING BEEN SET UP AND FORTIFIED OVER AND OVER AGAIN.
BREAKING THROUGH IT IS NO SMALL TASK.
...THE MAIN HOUSE DOES HAVE IMPREGNABLE DEFENSES.
AND ON TOP OF THAT, IT IS SUPPOSEDLY WELL KNOWN AS A SACRED MOUNTAIN SITE.
THE GREATER THE SPIRITUAL POWER OF THE LAND, THE STRONGER THE BARRIER.

SO, WHAT ARE YOU SAYING?

THAT'S IT? THERE'S NOTHING WE CAN DO ABOUT IT?

KATSU (TAK)

I WON'T ACCEPT THAT.

MY LORDS...
BE TRUE TO YOUR NAME—DURAS, THE PRIDEFUL ONES.

AND DO WHATEVER IT TAKES TO GET THE KEY OF ENOCH.

Story 47 · END

THE
BETRAYAL
KNOWS MY NAME

Story 48
RESIDENCE OF THE MAIN BRANCH OF THE GIOU, KYOTO
PITA (PAUSE)
...?
SOMETHIN' THE MATTER?
THIS MORNING, I THOUGHT I FELT THE AIR TREMBLE FOR A MOMENT...
....

...NO.
IT'S NOTHING—...
DODO (RUMBLE)
DO
DO
DO
Story 48
PERPLEX

HUFF
HUFF
HUFF,
DODO
DODO
SOME-HOW...
...WE'VE MANAGED TO LURE HIM DEEPER INTO THE MOUNTAINS...
...WITH-OUT EVEN KNOWING WHAT HE REALLY IS...
AN OPPONENT ON WHOM THE "CAGE OF BINDING" HAS NO EFFECT—
AND HE DIDN'T BREAK IT—HE JUST WALKED THROUGH IT LIKE NOTHING WAS THERE...! I'VE NEVER SEEN THAT BEFORE...
HE'S NOT POSSESSED BY A DEMON? AND HE'S NOT A DURAS? THEN WHAT IS HE...!!?

MY LEFT ARM IS WORSE THAN I THOUGHT.
POTATA (SPLISH)
AND I'VE GOT SOME BROKEN RIBS...
I'M PUTTING ALL THE POWER I CAN INTO HEALING, BUT IT WON'T WORK IN TIME.
COUGH
...AND TOOKO...
...IS A LITTLE BETTER OFF, BUT......
WE COMPLETELY MISCALCULATED AT THE START.
UNABLE TO DISMISS THE POSSIBILITY THAT OUR OPPONENT WAS A HUMAN BEING, WE SHRANK FROM FIGHTING HIM WITH OUR FULL STRENGTH.
AND THAT, RIGHT THEN, DECIDED THE BATTLE'S OUTCOME.
WHOEVER HESITATES EVEN THE TINIEST BIT WILL LOSE.
HE'S THAT SORT OF OPPONENT ......!!

—WHAT IF REIGA...
...JUST ATTACKED OUT OF NOWHERE? WHAT WOULD YOU DO WITHOUT ME THERE!?
NO MATTER WHAT HAPPENS TO US...
...DON'T EVER DOUBT.
DON'T LOSE SIGHT OF YOURSELF.
IF YOU CAN DO THAT...THEN... I WILL COME BACK TO YOU.
......HOTSUMA.
I BELIEVE IN YOU...!
—TOOKO.

IN THIS STATE, WE'RE NO MATCH FOR HIM...
!?
YOU JUMP INTO THE RIVER WHILE I LEAD HIM AWAY.
WH...
WHAT'S THAT GOING TO DO!?
YOU KNOW WHAT WE HAVE TO DO IN THESE SITUATIONS.
IF WE KEEP FIGHTING LIKE THIS, WE'RE BOTH DONE FOR.
MAKE SURE THE ONE WITH THE HIGHER CHANCE OF SURVIVING DOES SO.
......!!
CONSIDERING OUR INJURIES...
...THE ONE WITH ENOUGH STRENGTH LEFT TO WITHSTAND JUMPING OFF FROM HERE... IS YOU.
DODODO (RUMBLE)
DON'T TALK LIKE THAT! IT'S AWFUL...!!
YOU MAKE IT SOUND LIKE YOU'RE PLANNING TO DIE, SHUUSEI...!!

YOU REALLY THINK...
...I'LL GO WITHOUT A FIGHT?...
SHUU...
BLOOOOOOOD...!!
GOA (FWOOM)
ZA (KTCH)
...BLOOD
GASP

DON (BOOM)
ZAPAAAAN (KA-SPLAAASH)

GOBO (BUBBLE)
GOBO
GOBO
SHUUSEI ......!
—NO......
I HAVE TO STAY CONSCIOUS ...!
I WANT TO PROTECT...
I DON'T WANT ANYONE TO DIE.
I DON'T WANT... TO LOSE ANY-ONE...!

TSUKUMO...

YUKI-CHAN...

HOTSUMA......

EVERY-ONE!

HELP SHUUSEI!

MY FRIEND, MY DEAR FRIEND...

SAVE HIM!

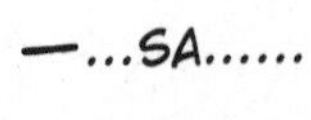

SAVE HIM ...!!
PI (BEEP)
PI
HFF...!
HFF...!
PI
PI
SIGN: CENTRAL HOSPITAL
中央病院
...WHERE AM I......?

HEY, EVERY-ONE!

THEY FOUND TOOKO-KUN!!

WE RECEIVED SOME INTEL THAT AN INJURED GIRL WAS TAKEN THERE AROUND DAWN—

...AND GOING BY HER PHYSICAL DESCRIPTION, IT HAS TO BE TOOKO-KUN.

HOTTSU AND THE OTHERS ARE HEADING THERE TO MAKE SURE!

—THEY FOUND...
...TOOKO-CHAN......
WE'LL GO STRAIGHT TO THE HOSPITAL FIRST TO MAKE SURE IT'S REALLY HER.
HER INJURIES AREN'T LIFE-THREATENING, BUT SHE'S STILL UNCONSCIOUS, THEY'RE SAYING.
THAT'S GREAT, TSUKUMO!
....
...IBUKI-SAN...
WHAT ABOUT SHUUSEI?

......
...UNFOR-TUNATELY...
...THERE IS STILL NO TRACE OF SHUUSEI-KUN.
......!
YOU JACK-ASS.
JUST BE HAPPY...
...THEY FOUND TOOKO!
...TOOKO'S OKAY.
SO SHUUSEI MUST BE OKAY TOO.

AND I WILL FIND HIM.
—......
HOTSUMA-KUN...
I APOLOGIZE, BUT I MUST LEAVE YOU HERE.
SOMEONE FROM THE MAIN FAMILY WILL MEET YOU HERE.
BURORO (VROOM)
SOMEONE FROM THE MAIN FAMILY...
WONDER WHO?
I'VE NEVER MET NY OF HEM FORE.
ZA (KTCH)
OTSUMAAA-CHAN! ♬
HYU (WHOOSH)

ZUGAAA (KA-CRASH)
GA (WHAM)
DOGO (BONK)
...HO-
HOTSUMA-KUN!!?

HA HA HA HA
YOUR BACK WAS WIDE OPEN, THERE! DUNCE!
...HEY!
BEEN A WHILE, TSUKUMO!
IT'S NICE TO SEE YOU, MASTER ROU.
ZAWA (MURMUR) ZAWA
ざわざわ…
H-HOTSUMA-KUN!
ARE YOU ALL RIGHT!?
BUCHI
......DAMMIT!
OLD FOGEY!!

HUNH!?
BYU (WOOSH)
HEY—
HEY!
NOW JUST A MIN-NIT!!
SONNY, ARE YOU SERI-OUSLY TRYIN' TO KNOCK AROUND YOUR OWN TEACHER !?
YOU HOLD UP!!
THAT'S TOUGH LOVE FOR YOU! DUNCE!
YOU WOULDA BROKEN SOME BONES IF I HADN'T DEFENDED OUT OF INSTINCT!!
YEAH, NO THANKS! QUIT DODGING ME! OLD FOGEY!!
'COURSE I'M GONNA DODGE!!
...THERE THEY GO AGAIN.
AGAIN ...?
ZARI! (KSTCH!)
YOU TWO IDIOTS OVER THERE—
STOP THAT THIS INSTANT!

ザッ
ZA (KTCH)
THIS IS A HOSPITAL!
YOU DON'T EVEN HAVE THE COMMON SENSE TO AT LEAST SAVE YOUR QUARRELS FOR AN APPROPRIATE LOCATION?
HONESTLY, BOTH STUDENT AND TEACHER...
...ARE A DISGRACE TO OUR CLAN.
ZUDO (STAB)
ひゅ~う
HYUUUU (WHOOSH)
DISGRACE, HE SAYS...
HIS TONGUE'S SHARPER THAN SHUUSEI'S......
THE ONE IN GLASSES...
...IS THE MASTER WHO TRAINED TOOKO-CHAN AND ME.
OH......!
THEIR MASTER...
THE ZWEILT OF THE MASTER CLASS WHO HAVE ABILITIES OCCASIONALLY COME TO OUR AID ON THE FRONT LINES.
SO...
...THAT'S WHO THESE PEOPLE ARE—...
ALL RIGHT.
IF YOU GOT THE WILL TO HIT ME BACK, YOU CAN COME WITH US!
WHA?
I WAS THINKIN' THAT IF YOU KEPT LOOKIN' SO GLOOMY, I'D JUST LEAVE YA HERE.

WELL, I GUESS YOU'RE LOOKIN' ALL RIGHT! YOU JUST BARELY PASSED THE TEST.
'COS YOU'D JUST GET IN THE WAY OF FINDIN' SHUUSEI!
GIGI CHNNNGH
WHO DIED AND MADE YOU KING!?
GI GI
...FIND HIM. YOU GOTTA.
HE'S YOUR PARTNER.
—
....
...COURSE I WILL!
...YOU MUST BE YUKI-SAMA?
Y...
YES, I AM!
FORGIVE US FOR NOT INTRODUCING OURSELVES SOONER. I AM SHIZUKA USUI.
AND THIS IS...
ROU REIZEN, HERE.
BORN AND RAISED IN KOBE! TWENTY-SEVEN AND SINGLE! AND TRAININ' MASTER TO HOTSUMA AND SHUUSEI! GOOD TO MEETCHA!

IT'S NICE TO MEET YOU TOO!
"USUI," HE SAID...
AND BY THE WAY—
SO HE'S SHUUSEI'S COUSIN. THEY DO LOOK ALIKE, DON'T THEY.
...HAVE YOU MET THESE TWO BEFORE, LUKA?
YES......
JUST ONCE.
A-HA!
—THIS ONE'S A RELATIVE OF SHUUSEI'S! A COUSIN, OR WHATNOT.
LOOKS LIKE HIM, DON'T HE?
WOULD YOU MIND NOT HANGING ALL OVER ME? IT'S STIFLING.
—YUKI-SAMA, LET'S HURRY UP AND GET TO THE HOSPITAL ROOM.
TIME IS OF THE ESSENCE.
......
...BUT I CAN TELL...
...THERE'S SOMETHING STRANGE ABOUT THEM.
WEARING LONG SLEEVES AND LAYERS...
...AND EVEN GLOVES...
NOW THAT YOU MENTION IT... YOU'RE RIGHT.
AND IT IS PRETTY HOT OUT—

—OH?
BUT SHUUSEI IS STILL MISSING...
WE CAN'T CELEBRATE YET.
...SO, YOU'LL BE GOING TO UENO PARK?
RIGHT. TO HELP PURIFY THE LAND...
WE'RE WAITING FOR THE RIDE NOW.
ONLY MORNING AND ALREADY WORKING HARD, EH?
...EXCEPT I WAS TOLD TO GO TO MY "REAL" JOB...
THOUGH FRANKLY THERE'S NO WAY I'M UP TO IT.
BUUUT IF YOU AREN'T THERE, RII-KUN, HOW WILL THEY BE ABLE TO DO THE SHOOT?
HMM...
THEY LET YOU GO, LIA, SO WHY IS SAIRI STILL TIED UP WITH ALL THAT?
OH— THAT'S 'COS...
...I WAS JUST ONE OF AN IDOL SINGER GROUP OF, LIKE, TWENTY GIRLS, SO IT WAS PRETTY EASY TO REPLACE ME.
BUT SAIRI'S AN ACTOR, SO, YOU KNOW...
OH, SO THAT'S WHAT'S GOING

...WE HAVE NO CHOICE BUT TO TRUST YUKI AND THE OTHERS TO FIND SHUUSEI.
YES. AND AT SOME POINT, I THINK...
...THEY'LL HAVE RII-KUN GO TO KYOTO, TO ERASE THE WITNESSES' MEMORIES.
OH, RIGHT... THOSE GIRLS WHO WERE ATTACKED BY THAT PSYCHOTIC MAN?
......WHAT ......!?
RIGHT. APPARENTLY THEY'RE QUITE DISTRESSED AND CON-FUSED...
...AND THE MEDICINE ISN'T HELP-ING ON ITS OWN......
PURURURU (RING RING)
HM?
PI (BIP)
IT'S THE COMMANDER. WHAT NOW?
HELLO? ...YES, SIR.
...YES, EVERYONE'S HERE.

....
...UNDER-STOOD.
PI (BIP)
DID SOMETHING HAPPEN?
—...IT HAPPENED AGAIN...
MORE VICTIMS FROM ENJU MIDDLE.
THIS TIME, THERE WERE TWO.
Story 48 • END

THE
BETRAYAL
KNOWS MY NAME

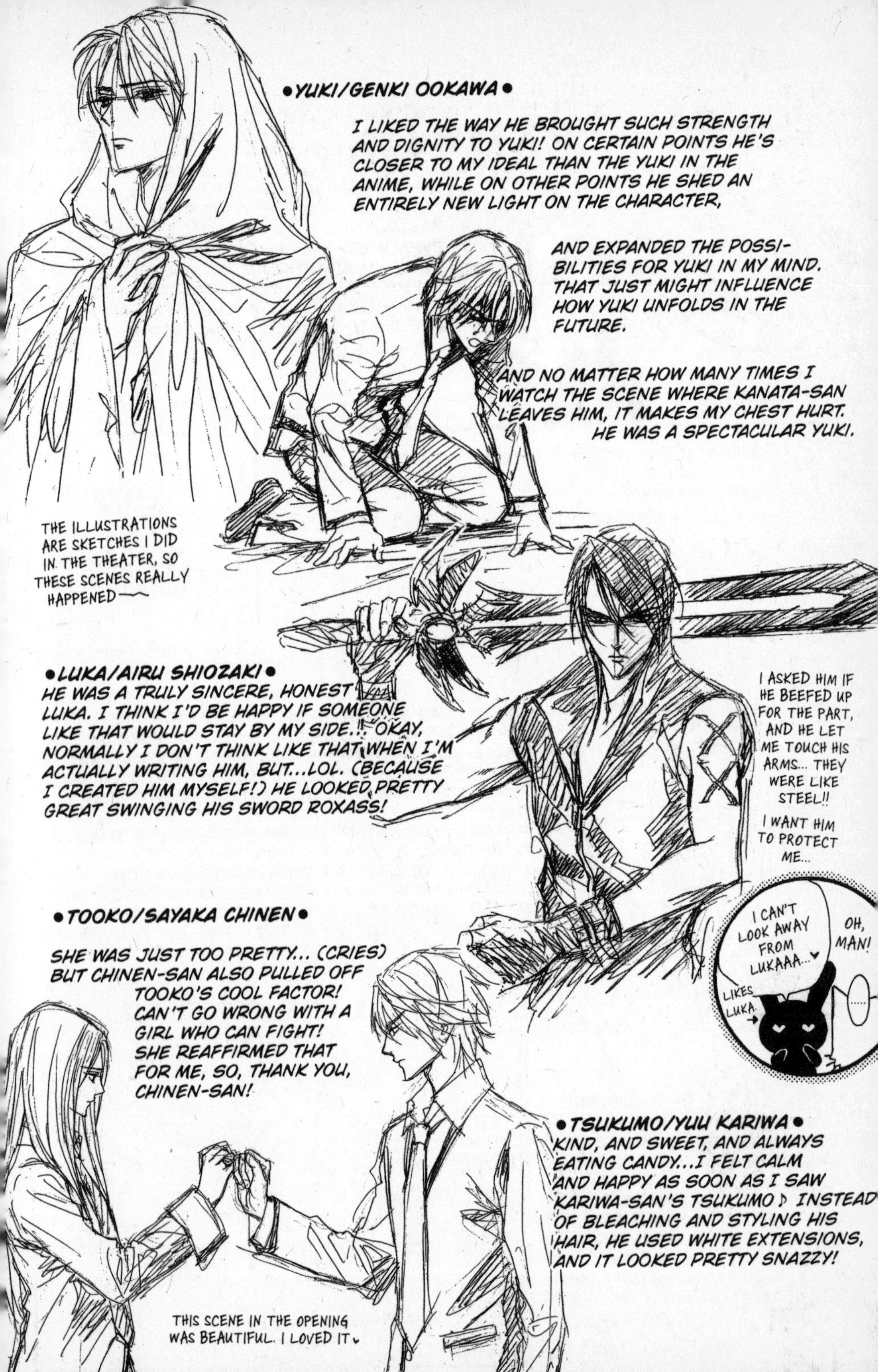

•YUKI/GENKI OOKAWA•
I LIKED THE WAY HE BROUGHT SUCH STRENGTH AND DIGNITY TO YUKI! ON CERTAIN POINTS HE'S CLOSER TO MY IDEAL THAN THE YUKI IN THE ANIME, WHILE ON OTHER POINTS HE SHED AN ENTIRELY NEW LIGHT ON THE CHARACTER,
AND EXPANDED THE POSSIBILITIES FOR YUKI IN MY MIND. THAT JUST MIGHT INFLUENCE HOW YUKI UNFOLDS IN THE FUTURE.
AND NO MATTER HOW MANY TIMES I WATCH THE SCENE WHERE KANATA-SAN LEAVES HIM, IT MAKES MY CHEST HURT. HE WAS A SPECTACULAR YUKI.
THE ILLUSTRATIONS ARE SKETCHES I DID IN THE THEATER, SO THESE SCENES REALLY HAPPENED—
•LUKA/AIRU SHIOZAKI•
HE WAS A TRULY SINCERE, HONEST LUKA. I THINK I'D BE HAPPY IF SOMEONE LIKE THAT WOULD STAY BY MY SIDE..! OKAY, NORMALLY I DON'T THINK LIKE THAT WHEN I'M ACTUALLY WRITING HIM, BUT...LOL. (BECAUSE I CREATED HIM MYSELF!) HE LOOKED PRETTY GREAT SWINGING HIS SWORD ROXASS!
I ASKED HIM IF HE BEEFED UP FOR THE PART, AND HE LET ME TOUCH HIS ARMS... THEY WERE LIKE STEEL!!
I WANT HIM TO PROTECT ME...
I CAN'T LOOK AWAY FROM LUKAAA...♥
OH, MAN!
LIKES LUKA.
•TOOKO/SAYAKA CHINEN•
SHE WAS JUST TOO PRETTY... (CRIES) BUT CHINEN-SAN ALSO PULLED OFF TOOKO'S COOL FACTOR! CAN'T GO WRONG WITH A GIRL WHO CAN FIGHT! SHE REAFFIRMED THAT FOR ME, SO, THANK YOU, CHINEN-SAN!
•TSUKUMO/YUU KARIWA•
KIND, AND SWEET, AND ALWAYS EATING CANDY...I FELT CALM AND HAPPY AS SOON AS I SAW KARIWA-SAN'S TSUKUMO ♪ INSTEAD OF BLEACHING AND STYLING HIS HAIR, HE USED WHITE EXTENSIONS, AND IT LOOKED PRETTY SNAZZY!
THIS SCENE IN THE OPENING WAS BEAUTIFUL. I LOVED IT ♥

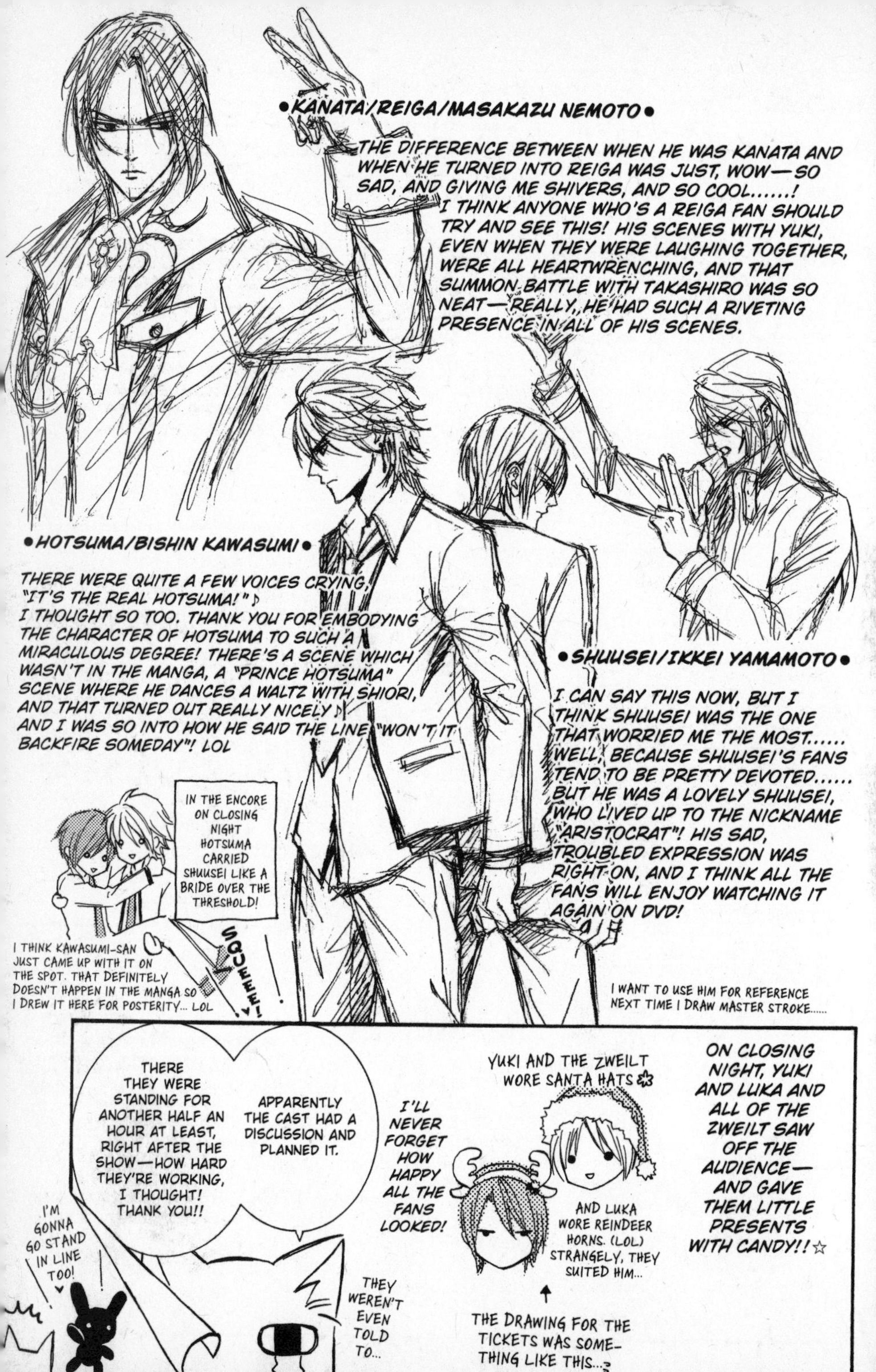
•KANATA/REIGA/MASAKAZU NEMOTO•
THE DIFFERENCE BETWEEN WHEN HE WAS KANATA AND WHEN HE TURNED INTO REIGA WAS JUST, WOW—SO SAD, AND GIVING ME SHIVERS, AND SO COOL......! I THINK ANYONE WHO'S A REIGA FAN SHOULD TRY AND SEE THIS! HIS SCENES WITH YUKI, EVEN WHEN THEY WERE LAUGHING TOGETHER, WERE ALL HEARTWRENCHING, AND THAT SUMMON BATTLE WITH TAKASHIRO WAS SO NEAT—REALLY, HE HAD SUCH A RIVETING PRESENCE IN ALL OF HIS SCENES.
•HOTSUMA/BISHIN KAWASUMI•
THERE WERE QUITE A FEW VOICES CRYING, "IT'S THE REAL HOTSUMA!"♪ I THOUGHT SO TOO. THANK YOU FOR EMBODYING THE CHARACTER OF HOTSUMA TO SUCH A MIRACULOUS DEGREE! THERE'S A SCENE WHICH WASN'T IN THE MANGA, A "PRINCE HOTSUMA" SCENE WHERE HE DANCES A WALTZ WITH SHIORI, AND THAT TURNED OUT REALLY NICELY♪ AND I WAS SO INTO HOW HE SAID THE LINE "WON'T IT BACKFIRE SOMEDAY"! LOL
•SHUUSEI/IKKEI YAMAMOTO•
I CAN SAY THIS NOW, BUT I THINK SHUUSEI WAS THE ONE THAT WORRIED ME THE MOST...... WELL, BECAUSE SHUUSEI'S FANS TEND TO BE PRETTY DEVOTED...... BUT HE WAS A LOVELY SHUUSEI, WHO LIVED UP TO THE NICKNAME "ARISTOCRAT"! HIS SAD, TROUBLED EXPRESSION WAS RIGHT ON, AND I THINK ALL THE FANS WILL ENJOY WATCHING IT AGAIN ON DVD!
IN THE ENCORE ON CLOSING NIGHT HOTSUMA CARRIED SHUUSEI LIKE A BRIDE OVER THE THRESHOLD!
SQUEEE!
I THINK KAWASUMI-SAN JUST CAME UP WITH IT ON THE SPOT. THAT DEFINITELY DOESN'T HAPPEN IN THE MANGA SO I DREW IT HERE FOR POSTERITY... LOL
I WANT TO USE HIM FOR REFERENCE NEXT TIME I DRAW MASTER STROKE......
ON CLOSING NIGHT, YUKI AND LUKA AND ALL OF THE ZWEILT SAW OFF THE AUDIENCE—AND GAVE THEM LITTLE PRESENTS WITH CANDY!!☆
YUKI AND THE ZWEILT WORE SANTA HATS✿
AND LUKA WORE REINDEER HORNS. (LOL) STRANGELY, THEY SUITED HIM...
I'LL NEVER FORGET HOW HAPPY ALL THE FANS LOOKED!
THE DRAWING FOR THE TICKETS WAS SOMETHING LIKE THIS...?
APPARENTLY THE CAST HAD A DISCUSSION AND PLANNED IT.
THERE THEY WERE STANDING FOR ANOTHER HALF AN HOUR AT LEAST, RIGHT AFTER THE SHOW—HOW HARD THEY'RE WORKING, I THOUGHT! THANK YOU!!
THEY WEREN'T EVEN TOLD TO...
I'M GONNA GO STAND IN LINE TOO!

EVERYONE IN THE SUPPORTING CAST TOO, WAS REALLY WONDERFUL, AND I WAS LEFT WITH A FEELING OF AWE THAT THERE ARE SO MANY TALENTED PEOPLE IN THIS WORLD. I'D LIKE TO WRITE MY IMPRESSIONS OF EACH AND EVERY ONE, BUT I WOULD JUST END UP CUTTING CORNERS DUE TO SPACE, SO I'LL LEAVE OFF THERE...

THERE WAS A LINE IN THE THEME SONG THAT WENT "THE BONDS TWISTED 'ROUND US, PAINFULLY TIGHT" AND I WAS SO IMPRESSED, BECAUSE THAT REALLY GETS TO THE CENTER OF WHAT THE WORLD OF URABOKU IS. I THINK I WAS PROBABLY THE MOST MOVED BY HOW THE "GOOD" POINTS OF URABOKU, THE PARTS THAT HIT HOME, THE LINES AND THE THEMES I WANTED TO COMMUNICATE, WERE ALL UP THERE INTERWOVEN SO PERFECTLY ON THE STAGE. I THINK THEY MUST HAVE APPROACHED THE STORY WITH A LOT OF PATIENCE TO MAKE SURE THEY BROUGHT ANOTHER PERSON'S WORK TO LIFE WITHOUT MISINTERPRETING ANYTHING. I'M TRULY FILLED WITH GRATITUDE.
TO ALL OF THE CAST, AND ALL OF THE STAFF, THANK YOU, THANK YOU, THANK YOU SO MUCH!!

THANKS TO THE SUPPORT OF EVERYONE WHO WENT TO SEE THE SHOW, THE SEQUEL WILL COME TO THE KICHIJOUJI ZENSHINZA THEATRE IN AUGUST! ♪
AND THEN, THE THIRD SHOW IS SET FOR NOVEMBER!!
PLEASE CHECK THE WEBSITE FOR DETAILS
IF YOU MISSED THE FIRST RUN, YOU CAN CATCH IT ON DVD~! ♥
→ IT WAS SO GOOD!
TO EVERYONE WHO COULDN'T MAKE IT BUT SHOWED THEIR SUPPORT, AND EVERYONE WHO SAID THEY'RE DEFINITELY GOING TO SEE THE SECOND RUN—THANKS TO ALL OF YOU TOO~
STAGE PRODUCTION PUBLIC WEBSITE (JAPANESE ONLY)
HTTP://WWW.URABOKU-STAGE.JP
THEY'RE ON TWITTER TOO. THEY'RE REALLY NICE. ♥
AND IN THE SECOND INSTALLMENT WE'LL FINALLY GET TO MEET KUROTO AND SENSHIROU!! IT'S LIKE A DREAM~♥ I CAN'T WAIT!!

ALSO...
I'M REALLY GRATEFUL FOR THE SUGGESTIONS OOKAWA-SAN GAVE ME ON THE DESIGN OF SAIRI'S AND LIA'S WEAPONS.
WHA? I DIDN'T KNOW YOU COULD DRAW SO WELL!
SHOULD I SAY THAT AS A MANGA ARTIST!?
THEY LOOK TOTALLY NEAT♪ AND THEY'VE ALREADY MADE AN APPEARANCE IN ASUKA, SO THAT SHOULD BE IN THE NEXT VOLUME. GET READY!!
AND THEN KAWASUMI-SAN PICKED OUT WHAT KIND OF CAR SAIRI SHOULD DRIVE, WHICH I WAS WORRYING ABOUT AT THE TIME...
IT HELPS TO TALK ABOUT THAT SORT OF THING...
YOU'VE ALL HELPED ME IN SO MANY WAYS! THANK YOU!!
AND LET ME RELAX TOO...

※ORDERS FOR THE LIMITED EDITION ARE NO LONGER BEING ACCEPTED.

OFF-SHOT CARD

↑ IN THE LIMITED EDITION

SO WE WERE ABLE TO PUT ONE IN THIS TIME TOO. (IT'S THE SIXTH CARD.) AT THE REQUEST OF THE BLACK BUNNY, I MADE IT SHUUSEI-KUN.

I HAD TO DO THE OFFSHOT CARDS FOR TWO COMIC VOLUMES (THE LIMITED EDITION AND THE NORMAL PAPERBACK) AND THE COLORING WAS JUST UNENDING.

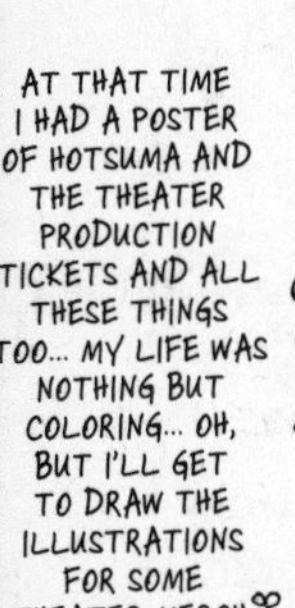

AT THAT TIME I HAD A POSTER OF HOTSUMA AND THE THEATER PRODUCTION TICKETS AND ALL THESE THINGS TOO... MY LIFE WAS NOTHING BUT COLORING... OH, BUT I'LL GET TO DRAW THE ILLUSTRATIONS FOR SOME THEATER MERCH.♡

IF YOU HAVE ANY REQUESTS FOR OFFSHOT CARDS, PLEASE DO LET ME KNOW.

SO AT LAST URABOKU HAS MADE IT TO TEN VOLUMES. I DIDN'T THINK ANYONE WOULD LET ME KEEP DRAWING IT FOR THIS LONG. IT'S ALL THANKS TO MY READERS. THANK YOU.

SO WITH THIS VOLUME THE STORY HAS FINALLY STARTED TO MOVE IN EARNEST, AND I'LL WORK HARD SO THAT YOU CAN KEEP READING IT. AND I'LL DO MY BEST TO MAKE ALL THE PLOT POINTS PILED UP IN MY HEAD UNFOLD SMOOTHLY...! LOL

SO, UNTIL WE MEET AGAIN.

THE LIMITED EDITION HAS METALLIC INK AND THINGS LIKE THAT, AND IT REALLY DID COME OUT AS SOMETHING SPECIAL. I'M GLAD WE PUT THIS OUT! ♪

BEHIND THE SCENES OF URABOKU - END

THE WEAPONS OF THE ZWEILT CAN ONLY BE USED BY THEIR OWNERS.
YAAAAAAAH!
IN VOLUME 7, THERE WAS A SCENE IN WHICH YUKI PICKED UP KUROTO'S SWORD AND ATTACKED WITH IT, BUT THE DURAS DIDN'T FALL. ANYONE ELSE WOULD HAVE HAD THE SAME RESULT. BUT WITH ONE'S OWN WEAPON, ONE HARDLY FEELS ITS WEIGHT AT ALL WHEN FIGHTING.

LUKA CAN EXTEND AND RETRACT HIS NAILS AT WILL.
SO HE NEVER HAS TO TRIM THEM! (LOL)
WOOOOW! JUST LIKE A KITTY!
※ BUT HE IS A DURAS.
NYU (SHP)

SPECIAL THANKS

✝

K-san
H.Sanbe
H.Matsuo
T.Kondo
R.Mozai

K.Okuda
E.Yamagishi

Y.Suzuki
K.Yamamoto

...... and You

PLEASE SEND YOUR COMMENTS AND OPINIONS...

HOTARU ODAGIRI
C/O GEKKAN ASUKA EDITING DEPARTMENT
KADOKAWA SHOTEN, INC.
TOKYO, JAPAN 102-8078

MY WEBSITE IS NOW A BLOG

HTTP://SEKAI-KAKERA.JUGEM.JP

PLEASE COME CHECK IT OUT! ♥

ONCE AGAIN, THANK YOU FOR ALL THE NEW YEAR'S GREETINGS AND VALENTINE'S DAY CHOCOLATES!

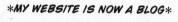

Translation Notes

Page 22
A red string has connotations of love and destiny, stemming from a cute superstition which says that soul mates are bound together by an invisible red string.

Page 36
Since Luka hails from Infernus, he is not terribly familiar with Japanese culture and pronounces *yukata* (a light summer kimono) with katakana in quotes in the Japanese edition of Volume 9.

Page 59
In this translation, Tachibana exclaims "Magnifeek!" upon seeing Luka in his yukata. In the original edition, he says "Excellent!" in Japanese-accented English.

Page 64
Wearing clothing of any kind into a Japanese bathhouse or hot spring is strictly forbidden. The Zweilt had every reason to expect that they would get to see Tachibana without a hat...but Tachibana is still being Tachibana.

Page 174
Due mainly to some Japan Railways ad campaigns in the '90s and the fact that New Year's Day is the major winter holiday in Japan, Christmas has taken on a romantic tone in the popular imagination there.

Page 185
Taitou City is not its own city but an area of Tokyo that receives the designation "city" in English.

Page 191
"Taking a flying leap off the Kiyomizudera stage" is an idiom in Japanese for taking drastic action. The original Kiyomizudera temple in Kyoto has a platform like a dancing stage, like the one here, built over a precipice. In real life, jumping from it would end rather badly, and the idiom's etymology is based on the image of a dramatic suicide.

Page 242
Sagano is an area of Kyoto noted for its beautiful mountain scenery.

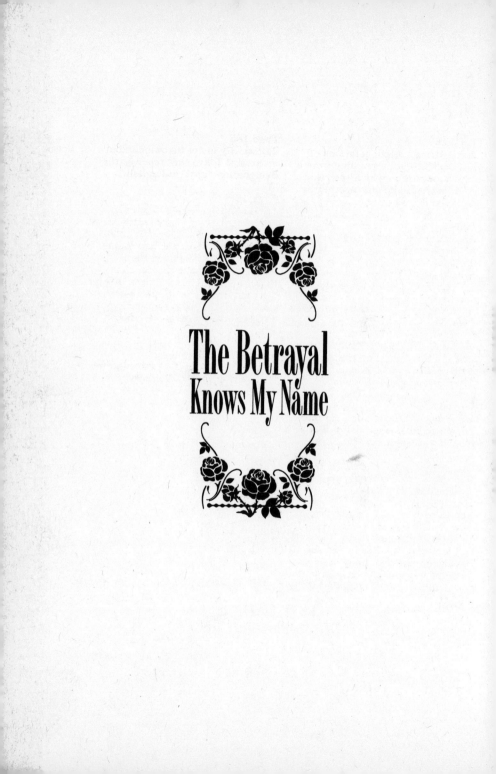

The Betrayal
Knows My Name

HOTARU ODAGIRI

Each day, after working on *Uraboku*, I collapse in an exhuasted heap. I have to wring every last drop of earnest feeling and sincerity from myself and pour it into this. Sometimes it feels like the burden of it will crush me. I used to think "I wish I could just work on this comfortably and not have to push myself so hard," but with this manga, that's a lost cause. So I guess I'll just strive to go as far as I can.

MESSAGE FROM VOLUME 9
(Japanese edition)

HOTARU ODAGIRI

As long as I'm alive,
I want to be of some good
to someone. But there's
really not much I can do.
Especially in hard times,
I have to remember to be
thankful for all I have, for
the kindness of others—
I know that, but when it
comes down to it, I'm unable
to hold on to that feeling.
That's the sort of year I've
had, always realizing that
I've still got quite a
ways to go.

MESSAGE FROM VOLUME 10
(Japanese edition)

THE BETRAYAL KNOWS MY NAME

HOTARU ODAGIRI

Translation: Melissa Tanaka † Lettering: Lys Blakeslee

Yen Press
Hachette Book Group
237 Park Avenue, New York, NY 10017

www.HachetteBookGroup.com
www.YenPress.com

Yen Press is an imprint of Hachette Book Group, Inc.
The Yen Press name and logo are trademarks of Hachette Book Group, Inc.

First Yen Press Edition: February 2013

ISBN: 978-0-316-23268-5

10 9 8 7 6 5 4 3 2

BVG

Printed in the
United States of America